Country Roads
~ of ~
OREGON

*A Guide Book
from Country Roads Press*

Country Roads
~ of ~
OREGON

Archie Satterfield

Illustrated by
Ned Schwartz

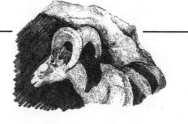

Country Roads Press
C A S T I N E • M A I N E

Country Roads of Oregon
© 1993 by Archie Satterfield. All rights reserved.

Published by Country Roads Press
P.O. Box 286, Lower Main Street
Castine, Maine 04421

Text and cover design by Edith Allard.
Library of Congress Catalog Card No. 93-070218
ISBN 1-56626-023-X

Printed in the United States of America.
10 9 8 7 6 5 4 3 2 1

To Bill McCarty

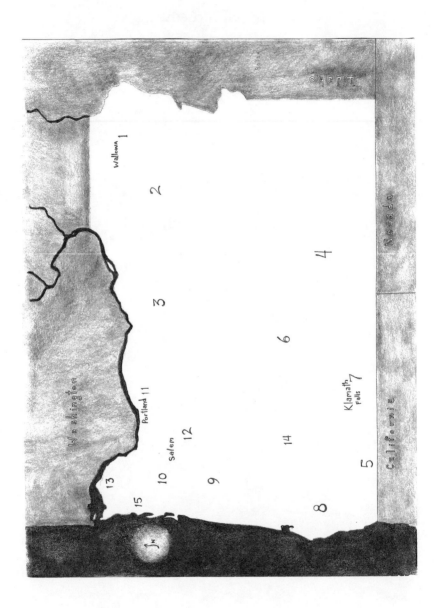

Contents

(& Key to Oregon Country Roads)

Introduction

One of the most challenging parts of writing this book was finding replacement words for "beautiful," "magnificent," "spectacular," "dramatic" and other superlatives that come to mind when describing Oregon. As the whole world surely knows by now, Oregon ranks high on the natural-beauty scale. Although I once lived in Oregon and recently had driven through much of the state writing travel articles, when I was researching this book I kept expecting to find some place that was a scenic ho-hum. If Oregon has such an area, I still haven't found it.

You can't go wrong driving on any road in Oregon, especially those that appear on maps as single red, black, or gray lines. (Oddly, the maps I bought don't have the blue lines made famous by William Least Heat Moon's *Blue Highways*.) Oregon's highways are so beautiful that even its two major interstates are pleasant experiences. In most parts of the country surveyors for the interstates were apparently required to find the most boring scenery they could: Remember John Steinbeck's lament in *Travels With Charlie* that the interstates made it possible to drive coast to coast without seeing a thing? Not so in Oregon. I-5 runs through the Willamette Valley and down through the Rogue River country. None of it bores me in the least. I-84 goes through the Columbia River Gorge before swinging southeast through Pendleton, La Grande, and Baker City. What more could we expect from a highway?

While it still surprises me that some people aren't impressed with vast open spaces where fence posts are the only vertical object in sight, I am as fond of the eastern Oregon desert as I am of the coastline and the Cascade Range. Compared to Washington, Oregon has suffered less from the effects of the so-called Cascade Curtain. Oregon seems to be much more cohesive than Washington, and I am convinced part of that happy circumstance can be credited to the *Oregonian,* which has always tried to be a regional rather than simply a Portland newspaper. Thus, I have found western Oregonians familiar and concerned with the entire state rather than only their local issues and scenery.

When I chose the roads to travel for this book, I first looked for routes that would represent each part of the state. After making my initial selection, I was pleased to find that they either connected with each other or were very close. This made it easy to present them in more or less the same sequence I drove them, beginning in the northeastern corner and working around the state in a clockwise fashion.

The reader will note that a great deal of diversity has resulted. Some roads have little or no services on them and tend to cover a lot of geography with only limited opportunities for shopping: You can't buy a thing on most of the road that follows the Rogue River to the ocean, and you have only one pit stop on the road I took from Burns to Plush. However, you have many opportunities to spend money on State 66 between Klamath Falls and Ashland, along the coast, and all through the Willamette Valley.

Some of these roads have been selected by the Bureau of Land Management (BLM) for inclusion in a system of National Backcountry Byways, which is described as a sister program to the National Scenic Byways program directed by the Forest Service. Both programs owe their birth to a study in 1987 which showed that 43 percent of Americans said driving for pleasure is one of their favorite forms of recreation.

One especially nice thing about traveling country roads in Oregon is that you can almost always find someone to talk to. The more remote the area, the longer you may have to talk to get information; first, you get acquainted, then ask the questions.

When you go driving in remote areas be sure you are prepared for emergencies. Carry all the emergency car repair items recommended by AAA (spare tire, tools, emergency kit, etc.) and always have a supply of water, food, and warm clothing. None of these roads is so remote that you will have to sit for days before someone comes along, but it could be a few hours between cars.

The most important factor for good country roading, I believe, is to travel with a good attitude: toward residents, fellow travelers, the environment, and yourself. Sports fishing enthusiasts insist that their hobby is better and cheaper than seeing a psychiatrist. That's the way I feel about exploring country roads.

To help clarify road designations, I've used the following abbreviations: I = interstate, US = US route or highway, and State = state route or highway.

Country Roads
~ of ~
OREGON

*A Guide Book
from Country Roads Press*

1 ~

Chief Joseph Country

From I-84 in La Grande take State 82 east to Enterprise and Joseph, then east on State 350 about eight miles to Forest Service Road 39. This leads south to Hells Canyon National Recreation Area and meets State 86 near Halfway, which in turn leads to I-84 again at Baker City.

Highlights: *Magnificent mountain scenery, hay meadows with streams running through them, farm and ranch towns with museums, art galleries, gift shops, a major foundry, feed stores, downhome cafes, Hells Canyon, and the Oregon Trail. It has been nominated for a National Scenic Byways designation by the Bureau of Land Management.*

The Wallowa area is such a beautiful end-of-the-road kind of place that nearly everyone who visits it comes to think of it as their own personal secret. My first visit was when my children were reaching high school age, a period when friends and prestige are more important than family outings. It rained the entire week we camped at the foot of Wallowa Lake, another sure-fire ingredient for a rotten time with four children, but everyone had a wonderful time and fifteen years later they still speak of the trip with a trace of nostalgia.

The Wallowa Valley is a Shangri-la place with a baled hay and saddle soap tang. Its broad valleys are laced with creeks and small rivers, and they in turn are framed by dramatic mountains. Stand in the middle of the valley and you see mountains in every direction, yet the valley is so large that you don't feel claustrophobic or trapped. Few lakes anywhere in the world have a more photogenic setting than Wallowa Lake, the valley's centerpiece, nestled right up against the mountains of the Eagle Cap Wilderness Area.

This loop trip has so many beautiful settings that you think you've seen about everything the valley can offer before you get to the lake. When you leave it to drive south into Hells Canyon you expect a visual letdown, but it doesn't happen. Be careful that this trip doesn't spoil you for the rest of the country roads described here.

Start by turning off I-84 to State 82 in the middle of La Grande, a ranch and farming town named by a French Canadian voyageur who reportedly exclaimed, "La grande!" ("How beautiful!") when he looked down into the valley. From La Grande, drive through Island City, practically a suburb of La Grande, then across flat farmland surrounded by low mountains. You will pass a few clusters of old farmhouses, some so weathered that they could be mistaken for pioneer museums.

Imbler is an elderly town with a few authentic false-front buildings and some attractive brick homes along the main street, which is also the highway. Imbler has virtually no services for visitors but is a good place to stop on a hot day for a cool sip in a cafe.

Shortly after leaving Imbler you will be near the low mountains on the east side of the valley that are topped with a thin fringe of timber. Wheat fields climb up the sides until it becomes too steep for tractors and combines. Most of the flat valleys are dedicated to row crops and alfalfa.

Elgin is another farm and ranch town with one or two cafes and a modest motel a block off the main drag. It also has a scattering of galleries and shops that showcase local artisans, many of whom work in wood and leather. The town's centerpiece is the historic Elgin Opera House/City Hall where the jail and library once shared quarters.

The Grande Ronde River runs through town, and some river-runners launch their kayaks and inflatables here. The river is quite tame at this point, but when it enters the Blue Mountains to the northeast it becomes extremely crooked. Its canyon through the Blue Mountains, from Troy down to the Snake River, is very steep and remote.

The Flight of the Nez Perce

State 82 begins climbing modestly just outside Elgin and goes over Minam Summit (3,638 feet) before dropping down to the town of Minam and the northern end of the Wallowa Valley. The grade between Minam and Wallowa was known for years as "Old Joseph's Deadline" for the Nez Perce Indian chief, father of the more famous Chief Joseph who led his people on the famous retreat toward Canada. The elder Joseph had been chief of a small band for many years, and they lived peacefully in the beautiful valley, even after the whites began encroaching in the 1860s in spite of a treaty signed in 1855 giving them the entire valley. The whites drew up a new treaty with new boundaries that drastically reduced the Nez Perce land. When the chiefs of the five local bands refused to sign, the whites appointed new chiefs and forced them to sign. This caused the elder Chief Joseph to build a series of rock cairns with ten-foot poles along the Minam grade as the boundary of his tribal land.

When he died, his son, also named Joseph, became chief. His relations with the white newcomers were also cordial at first, and members of both races respected the other's property boundaries. That changed when President Ulysses Grant waffled. First he signed an equitable executive order dividing the valley, then under pressure from unscrupulous Oregon politicians, signed a new order rescinding the property division. Even after this, the whites and Indians still managed to live in peace in the remote valley. It ended when someone in President Grant's administration told the Army on May 17, 1877, to move the Wallowa Nez Perce to the Lapwai Reservation in Idaho no later than June 15.

Chief Joseph asked for a delay until fall so his people could round up their livestock grazing in the mountain pastures and gather food for the winter. The Army refused, and tempers wore thin on both sides. The inevitable gunshot was fired by a white man who killed a Nez Perce over a property dispute. The Nez Perce people retaliated, and the war was on.

Chief Joseph, who was not one of the war chiefs, gathered his people and began a dash for Canada, which they called the Old Woman's Country in honor of Queen Victoria, knowing they would be safe there among their friends. This retreat has been called one of the greatest examples of military leadership in history. Chief Joseph's band had only a few men of fighting age but many elderly people, women, and children, some of whom were decrepit and ill. Joseph outmaneuvered the U.S. Army all along the way, but the 1,300-mile trek was finally too much for his people; some had died enroute and others became ill. The children were crying from hunger and the misery of the flight, so Chief Joseph at last, heartbreakingly, had to surrender when they were only about fifty miles from the safety of the Canadian border. There he gave a speech that contained the now-famous words: "From where the sun now stands I will fight no more forever."

Although Chief Joseph is one of the most revered men in Northwest history, by Indians and whites alike, he was never permitted to return to his beloved Wallowa Valley. He and his band were placed on the Colville Reservation in northern Washington. He was buried there in 1904, and people of all races make pilgrimages to his grave.

The elder Joseph's grave in the Wallowa Mountains was vandalized and his bones scattered, but more sensitive residents gathered them up, established a small park in his honor at the north end of his beloved Wallowa Lake, and buried his bones there.

The small, unpretentious town of Lostine, hardly more than a grocery store and tavern, is the first on entering the valley, and it also serves as the northern entryway into the Eagle Cap Wilderness. Several outfitters offer horseback trips into the backcountry.

Enterprise and Joseph are about evenly divided between agriculture and tourism, with the latter steadily gaining in importance. Within the modern American dream of making every town a tourist destination, these two towns have a distinct advantage because their setting is so beautiful and they are reasonably remote. The Chamber of Commerce is fond of calling the area the "Switzerland of America," but the softly rolling name, Wallowas (rhymes with "allow was"), has come to have its own visual image of mountains rising above the southern end of the lake and lush valleys with streams meandering through them.

Enterprise is the largest town in the valley and is headquarters for the Forest Service and the county government. It has a few clean and inexpensive motels, one or two good restaurants, and several craft and antique shops.

Don't miss Valley Bronze in Joseph, a world-class foundry where some major pieces of western art are cast. One example is the work of David Manuel, who has done many statues of the late John Wayne. The Wallowa County Museum in Joseph emphasizes Nez Perce and pioneer ranch artifacts.

Wallowa Lake begins on the southern end of Joseph, and here you'll see the signature scene of the Wallowas—the view down the lake to the mountains behind. Chief Joseph's grave

Wallowa Lake, one of Oregon's most beautiful places

is here, and the view is always inspiring. The road follows the eastern shore of the lake to Wallowa Lake State Park, one of the most beautiful parks in Oregon.

In addition to the camping, hiking, boating, and fishing for which the lake is so well known, it is also the site of the Mount Howard Aerial Tramway, which operates during the summer months and takes you on a twenty-minute ride from lake-level to the top of 8,256-foot Mount Howard. From there you can see in all directions: south into the Eagle Cap Wilderness, east into Idaho, and north and west into the Blue Mountains. Directly below you will see Wallowa Lake and the valley stretching off to the north.

The next leg of this loop trip begins in downtown Joseph where State 350 heads due east. It eventually dead-ends on the edge of Hells Canyon National Recreation Area beyond the community of Imnaha, but for the purposes of this trip, go eight miles from Joseph and turn south on Forest Service Road 39 and follow it through the mountains for sixty-two miles to Halfway.

Like so many logging roads in Oregon, Road 39 is paved and for the most part is in good condition. It is always wise to inquire about its condition from the Forest Service office in Enterprise. A number of primitive Forest Service campgrounds are spotted along the route, along with turnouts for views of the mountains surrounding Hells Canyon.

The road is crooked and steep in many places, and some motorhomes and most trailers will have difficulty making the turns and grades. It alternates between thick forest and open hillsides with broad views, and eventually ends when it meets State 86 on the southern end of Hells Canyon National Recreation Area. Here you can turn east on State 86, follow the Pine Creek to the Oxbow Dam, cross the Snake River into Idaho, and go on downriver a short distance to Homestead.

State 86 is a wider and better marked highway, and it takes you over the last ridges of the Wallowa Mountains until suddenly you begin a long, curving downhill descent in timberless country and far below you is a big valley with hay fields and row crops. Soon you will see the town of Halfway in the middle of the lush valley. This agricultural town is a good place to stop for an unpretentious meal in one of the cafes where the locals gather for coffee breaks, meals, and to exchange lots of good-natured insults.

Soon after leaving Halfway, the highway begins climbing and crosses a 3,653-foot summit before the small town of Richland, then crests a lower summit, 2,589 feet, before you arrive at Flagstaff Hill five miles from Baker City. Here the Bureau of Land Management's National Historic Oregon Trail Interpretive Center opened in 1992 and became known as one of the best of the series of such centers along the trail, which runs from the Missouri River at St. Joseph, Missouri, to Oregon City in Oregon's Willamette Valley.

Between 1841 and 1869, the 2,000-mile trek over this trail brought some 300,000 immigrants to the West Coast, making it the greatest peacetime migration in world history. Although many went into California—the gold rush of 1849 brought enormous numbers across the plains—the Oregon Country was more or less the official goal of the migration. Years later when historians and newspaper reporters interviewed the elderly trail veterans, to almost everyone's surprise the most common reason for leaving the Midwest for the Oregon Country was health. Everyone believed it was healthier out West.

Many immigrants walked the entire distance, not only to make it easier for the oxen or draft horses pulling the wagons, but because it was much more comfortable to walk than ride wagons with little or no shock-absorbing capacity. Speaking from experience as a child in the Ozarks, the author can assure you that sitting on a wooden seat in an iron-tired wagon going over rocks is what he would imagine it feels like to sit on a jackhammer.

The interpretive center on Flagstaff Hill has a large display area for artifacts from the trail and outside has a replica of a wagon train encampment. Paved walking trails lead to actual wagon ruts of the trail and scenic overlooks showing the kind of rough country the travelers had to cross without benefit of roads, motels, and restaurants.

In the Area

All numbers are within area code 503.

Wallowa County Chamber of Commerce, PO Box 427
    (Enterprise) 97828: 426-4622

Wallowa-Whitman National Forest, PO Box 907 (Baker) 97814: 523-6391

Eagle Cap Ranger District, PO Box M (Enterprise) 97828: 426-3104

Hells Canyon National Recreation Area, PO Box 490 (Enterprise) 97828: 426-4978

Wallowa Lake Tourist Committee, PO Box 853 (Joseph): (No phone)

Valley Bronze, PO Box 669 (Joseph) 97846: 432-7445

Wallowa Lake Tramway: 432-5331

Baker City Chamber of Commerce, 490 Campbell Street (Baker City) 97814: 523-3356 or (800) 523-1235

Oregon Trail Museum, 2490 Grove Street (Baker City) 97814: 523-9308

Flagstaff Hill National Historic Oregon Trail, PO Box 987 (Baker City) 97814: 523-1843

2 ~

The

Elkhorns

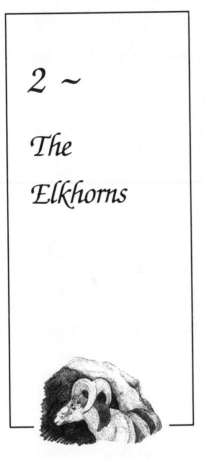

From **I-84** in Baker City, take State 7 west to Sumpter and Granite and continue on the route marked by Elkhorn Scenic Byway signs back to Baker City, or catch I-84 at North Powder.

Highlights: *Mountain scenery, Baker City, rivers and lakes, ghost towns, dredge tailings, rides on steam train, and wildlife refuges.*

In spite of the Oregon Trail connection and the town being on the natural transportation corridor, Baker City was created by gold found in the nearby Elkhorn mountains. It quickly outgrew its neighbors and in 1868 acquired the county seat the old-fashioned western way: A group of citizens hitched a team of horses to a wagon, drove over to the county seat at Auburn, stole all the county records, brought them to Baker City, and that was that. Auburn soon disappeared from the map.

Baker City has one of Oregon's best collections of ornate Victorian buildings; more than 100 of them are on the National Register of Historic Places, making it one of Oregon's several authentic pioneer towns. Unlike its neighboring states, Washington and California, Oregon has not yet been afflicted with the theme-town epidemic. If its towns look western, that is because they have always been that way. Few have had new identities painted on.

The Oregon Trail has become important to Baker City, and today it has its own Oregon Trail Regional Museum downtown, with a few relics found along the trail: pioneer clothing and furniture, large gold nuggets found in the area, and one of the best collections of rocks, minerals, and semi-precious stones in the West.

State 7 west from Baker City is beautiful any time of the year, but especially so in the spring and fall when the decidu-ous trees and low brush have their most vivid colors. In the autumn western larches turn color and lose their needles, too, which has caused more than one out-of-state tourist to as-sume the forest has been attacked by some terrible blight that is causing the trees to die. (Unfortunately, in the Elkhorn area the forest actually was attacked by beetles a few years ago and pine trees died by the millions.)

This loop trip follows the Powder River along the edge of the narrow river valley, twisting and turning with the topog-raphy rather than bulldozing through to make it straight, level, and boring. State 7 is the kind you will want to drive slowly so you can savor its pastoral beauty; it is one of those routes that brings to mind the word "motoring" rather than simply "driving."

One of the first places to turn off is at the Forest Service's Union Creek campground on Phillips Lake, just upstream from the earthen dam. The lake is stocked with largemouth bass, rainbow trout, and coho salmon.

After about thirty miles of ranch and mountain scenery, the BLM's Elkhorn Scenic Byway route leaves State 7 to follow the Powder River north on a paved county road toward Sumpter. Immediately after turning on this narrower highway, you will see the mounds of spoils from the gold dredges that churned up virtually every square foot of the Powder River Valley from here to Sumpter.

Gold was taken from the area by pan and rocker box as early as the 1850s, then the dredges arrived and worked off and on from 1913 until 1954, when the last dredge shut down for the last time and was left where it breathed its last, on the outskirts of Sumpter. During that forty-year period more than $10 million in gold, based on the old price of about $35 an ounce, was taken from the valley. At today's prices of more than $300 an ounce, the figure would be close to a billion dollars.

The whole valley looks something like a rock quarry with some brush beginning to grow back on the mounds. About halfway up the valley, surrounded by piles of the dredge spoils, are the Oregon Wildlife Commission's Wildlife Habitat and the Sumpter Valley Railroad. During the summer months the narrow-gauge railroad, dubbed the "Stump Dodger," runs a steam train powered by a wood-burning engine through the valley past nesting ducks, Canada geese, beaver, muskrat, elk, and deer. The track lacks a roundhouse so the engine pulls the cars for seven miles, then pushes them backward in the other direction.

The town of Sumpter is at the head of the valley where Cracker Creek enters the Powder River. The old dredge, steadily disintegrating, sits at the edge of the small, rustic town. Sumpter was founded in 1861 by a group of men who sympathized with the Confederacy, and they called it Fort Sumter in honor of the South Carolina fort where the first battle of the Civil War was fought in April of that year. The Post Office Department, very much a Union bureaucracy,

Sumpter dredge

wouldn't permit the rebels to celebrate the Union's first defeat in this manner. Fort was dropped from the name, and a "p" added to create Sumpter.

A decade later Chinese miners came in and reworked the same deposits in the valley, earning a good living in the process, while the Caucasian miners kept looking for new deposits. They found them. The best deposits were found lodged in the hillsides and that brought hardrock mining to the area as they dug tunnels and shafts, following the seams of gold.

By 1900 Sumpter had five hotels, an opera house, and some 3,000 citizens, and the deep mines and dredges were operating around the clock. Town fires seemed to be inevitable in the West during the nineteenth century, and Sumpter had its share of them, which helps explain why so few buildings remain today.

During these bonanza years, Sumpter was literally surrounded by mines with colorful names such as Goldbug-

Grizzly, May Queen, Baby McKee, and Belle of Baker. As with nearly all gold-rush towns, Sumpter's fall came on swift wings. When researchers for the WPA guidebook drove through in the early 1930s, one sentence described the town vividly: "Pack rats live in the vaults of two former banks."

This situation changed again when the gigantic dredge you see today was assembled and began crunching and grinding its way up the Powder River Valley, bringing steady, salaried jobs with it until the gold petered out, and the dredge was shut down forever in 1954.

Today Sumpter's population is around 100. It has a cluster of stores and its own post office. Its restaurants and stores have typically colorful names—Sumpter Nugget Restaurant, Elkhorn Saloon, One-Eyed Charlie's Broiler—and a scattering of antique stores with names such as The Black Market Antiques and Olde Assayers, a bed and breakfast, and two RV parks. Many of the mining claims are still being worked, and a few people live there and commute to work in the Baker City area. The dredge is slowly disintegrating, but the dry climate ensures that it will be there for our grandchildren to see.

From Sumpter a washboardy dirt road follows Cracker Creek six miles to the ghost town of Bourne, while the main Elkhorn route continues on pavement another sixteen miles to Granite.

If the correct definition of a ghost town is "one that is only a shadow of its former self," then Granite is a ghost town. It is a haphazard group of buildings scattered across an open slope overlooking the valley, and some of the decaying buildings look almost as though they were dropped off the back of a truck and haven't been touched since.

However, several families do live in the area, as proved by a long row of mailboxes in what was the heart of down town Granite in days gone by. Residents have gone to the trouble of placing small signs on empty buildings telling their former purpose.

In the 1960s Granite had a population of exactly one person named Ote Ford. He told a newspaper reporter that he once had two neighbors, but the mayor hung himself and the other, named Cliff the Prospector, left town to hunt for gold. So Ote became the mayor, council, and treasurer as well as the constituency. He said Granite was Republican and grumbled that "There's no such thing as isolation. Too many people want to share it with you." He wouldn't like the town a bit now.

Elkhorn National Scenic Byway continues north from Granite for fifty-seven miles to Haines on US 30. The remainder of the drive is over a road that is sometimes rough but always scenic. It occasionally touches on edges of the North Fork of the John Day Wilderness, and all of it is through Wallowa-Whitman National Forest land, which means that you should always be on the lookout for logging trucks. During deer and elk hunting season, you will see lots of pickups with rifle racks across the rear window.

During winter the Anthony Lakes Ski Area west of North Powder is popular with both downhill and cross-country skiers, snowmobilers, and sled-dog enthusiasts. It has a base elevation of 7,100 feet and has a day-lodge, cafeteria, lounge, and coffee shop. For summer visitors, the area has several hiking trails that lead off the road into the backcountry.

In the Area

All numbers are within area code 503.

Sumpter Valley Railroad, PO Box 389 (Baker City) 97814: 894-2268 or (800) 523-1235

Eastern Oregon Visitors Association, 490 Campbell Street (Baker City) 97814: 523-3356 or (800) 962-3700

Baker Ranger District, Route 1, Box 1 (Baker City) 97814: 523-6391

Bureau of Land Management, Baker Resource Area, PO Box 987 (Baker City) 97814: 523-6391

3 ~

The John Day Country

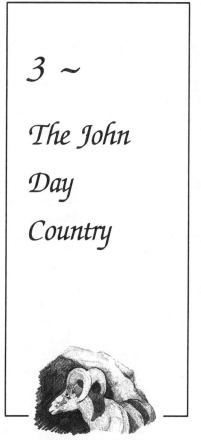

From I-84 at Baker City take State 7 west and follow signs to Austin Junction, where it joins US 26. Follow it west to Prineville.

Highlights: *Mountain and river canyon topography, cattle country, multicolored hills and fossils in the national monument, semi-arid climate, Kam Wah Chung & Co. Museum in John Day, and Prairie City Depot Park and Museum.*

You can't go wrong traveling on US 26 anywhere in Oregon. It begins at Astoria, follows the coast to Seaside, then swings inland and goes through just about everything Oregon has to offer in scenery and climate. This trip runs west from Baker City on State 7 until it joins US 26 at Austin and ends at Prineville. It overlaps part of the Elkhorn trip described earlier.

A short distance past the Sumpter turnoff, the highway begins a steady climb until it peaks at the 5,082-foot Larch Summit, then drops down on a gently winding route to level out at the remains of Whitney. The scattering of wooden buildings on the south side of the highway is worth a stop and perhaps a photo or two, because you'll never find a more convenient ghost town.

Whitney was a logging center when the railroad ran through between Baker City and Prairie City. The town's first death knell sounded when the mill burned in 1918. It staged a comeback for five years when the Oregon Lumber Company built another mill in 1939, but it was only a temporary respite because the mill closed when the company cut all the timber on a block of land it had purchased. When the railroad shut down in 1947, so did Whitney, this time for good. A dozen or so buildings remain, some used for storage while others just stand around looking forlorn and photogenic.

The road begins a steady climb again to the top of Tipton Summit (5,124 feet) just before dropping down to Austin Junction, where you will join US 26. Austin Junction has the dubious distinction of sometimes being the coldest place in the state.

US 26 is a favorite route for RVers, so be patient and expect slow traffic when going up long grades, such as the climb to the summit of Dixie Pass (5,279 feet). Soon after topping this pass, the landscape opens up dramatically, as if pulling a curtain aside, and stretched out for many miles before you is open country with a town far below, looking like the opening credits for a movie about the westward migration. The town is Prairie City, and its appearance in the middle of the open country saves you the trouble of wondering how it got its name.

On the way down to Prairie City you will note several "sets" of hills south of the valley, each set of hills a little higher than the last, until they finally become the Strawberry Range. The highest peak you will see is 9,000-foot Strawberry Mountain.

Prairie City is a friendly, unpretentious town. If you want brochures on the area you'll find them in a rack halfway back in the old, high-ceilinged hardware store. Prairie City began its life as a mining camp about two miles up Dixie Creek from its present site. It was a such a haphazard, wide-open temporary place that it was never platted. Cooler heads arrived and when the gold petered out, the present town was built where both Dixie Creek and Strawberry Creek enter the John Day River. It was given a post office in 1870. The Sumpter Valley Railroad tracks began hauling gold ore, cattle, logs, and passengers from Baker City in 1909.

A notable collection of pioneer artifacts is housed in the ten-room DeWitt Museum, the former railway station that has been restored and placed on the National Register of Historic Places. This is where the collection of Gail and Peacha DeWitt is housed. When the ranch couple began collecting pioneer artifacts and couldn't seem to stop, the community eventually pitched in and built a small museum for the collection. Then the railroad station was renovated and the collection moved there. In addition to ranching and gold-rush items, the museum also has an extensive collection of Chinese articles (when the 1870 census was taken of Prairie City, 219 of the 523 residents were Chinese). If you need to stretch your legs, the old track bed has been cleared, and you can walk the entire fifty-five miles, or sections thereof, back to Sumpter on the level roadbed.

John Day is the next town and like so many towns in eastern Oregon, nearly everyone in Oregon, if not the entire Northwest, is as familiar with its existence as they are with Portland. In John Day's case, it is in part due to the national monument that shares the same name. The whole region, however, is known as John Day Country and has come to represent rugged countryside with colorful hills and swift rivers.

The man who left his name on the region lived an incredibly rigorous life and died tragically. He was a Virginian who became a trapper on the Missouri River, then signed on with the John Jacob Astor party going overland to the mouth of the Columbia. Day almost died of exposure and starvation on the way across the mountains and was saved by a band of Indians who took him in until he recovered. When he finally did reach Astoria, he became mentally deranged and died. Oddly, John Day never saw the area named for him. In his travels and travails, he didn't stray far from the Snake River, which was his party's route to Astoria.

The town of John Day is the home of the Kam Wah Chung & Co. Museum, one of Oregon's best-known museums and perhaps the best collection of pioneer Chinese culture outside San Francisco. The building was a trading post for the military road built through the area in 1866, but was later sold to two Chinese merchants, Ing Hay and Lung On. The partners sold groceries, mining supplies, food imported from China, bootleg whiskey during Prohibition, and whatever else the Chinese community wanted. The building was also a community center and was used for religious services.

Its other important function was as the medical office of Ing "Doc" Hay, who was famous for his "pulse diagnosis." It was said he could diagnose many ailments by lightly feeling the patient's pulse.

In Chinese, Kam Wah Chung means "the golden flower of prosperity" and many of the Chinese did indeed prosper during the last two decades of the nineteenth century and well into the twentieth. The contributions of the Chinese in John Day is commemorated the first weekend in June with the Kam Wah Chung Days festival.

For eight miles west of John Day US 26 and the north-south US 395 run together, so traffic is quite heavy most of the year. The Clyde Holliday State Park is about six miles west of John Day and offers a place to camp or stop for a picnic. Once you reach the small, tidy town of Mount Vernon, US 395 continues on its northerly direction, leaving US 26 with about half the traffic.

The highway follows the John Day River down the valley through the small, picturesque town of Dayville, not much more than a place to stop for gas, a snack, and photos of the old frame buildings that reflect the ranching heritage of the valley. The highway gradually narrows into a deep canyon justifiably named Picture Gorge, then enters the Sheep Rock unit of the John Day Fossil Beds National Monument.

This monument, divided into three units—Sheep Rock, Painted Hills, and Clarno—is one of the more unusual monuments in the National Park system. Created in 1974, it covers 14,000 acres and is a laboratory for fossilized remains of plants and animals dating back at least sixty-five million years. Many of the fossilized animals found have no living descendants, such as the Telmatherium and the Hemipsalodon. Others that have relatives still with us include the Diceratherium, a relative of the rhinoceros, and the Hypertragulus, a mouse-deer that has relatives in Asia and Africa. Unlike many similar areas, the fossil beds are equally important for the study of the volcanic eruptions that occurred after the Cascade Range was created by an upheaval and the succession of ice ages that helped scour the mountains of lava and ash to expose the fossils.

Each unit has its own distinct features. Sheep Rock, which has the main information center, is the best place to see fossils because so many have been collected and placed on exhibit in the visitor center. (Visitors are prohibited from collecting fossils.) You can also walk along the 200-yard trail that leads from the information center to Sheep Rock Overlook, or take other trails through the park.

The next unit is Painted Hills, nine miles from Mitchell on US 26. This is the most spectacular of the three units. It is

notable for its enormous mounds of volcanic ash, some of which are almost perfect cones, layered with varying colors—red, pink, gold, bronze, and a sooty black—caused by the minerals in the ash. The colors are most brilliant in the early morning and late evening light and just after a rain. Photographers come from all over the world and spend several days, sometimes a few weeks, capturing the mounds in their various moods. Most prefer to work in the spring when wildflowers carpet the valley floor around the colorful hills.

You can tour the site by car, following a one-way paved loop road with turnouts and parking lots at the most advantageous sites, and you can walk along marked trails among the vivid hills.

Clarno is the third unit and is separated from the other two. Its main feature is an eroded ancient mudslide that shows many plant fossils, including parts of an ancient forest.

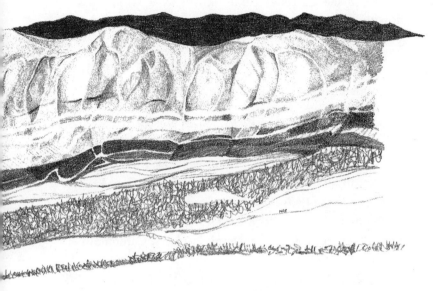

The colored cliffs at John Day Fossil Beds

It has two trails, each one-fourth mile long, that lead past fossils preserved in cliffs. As with the other units, it has a picnic area and restrooms. To reach the Clarno unit, you must drive a considerable distance north from the Painted Hills on State 207, turning west to the town of Fossil, and continuing twenty miles west on State 218.

The John Day River is left behind when you clear the 4,382-foot Keyes Creek Summit and descend to Mitchell, as the landscape opens to reveal the country of central Oregon with the Cascade Range as a backdrop. Off to the southwest you will see the Three Sisters due west of Bend, all three just over 10,000 feet. A bit south of them is Broken Top, barely over 9,000 feet.

Once the Cascades come into view, it is only a short downhill drive into Prineville, described in the next chapter.

In the Area

All numbers are within area code 503.

Grant County Chamber of Commerce, 281 West Main Street (John Day) 97845: 575-0546

Bureau of Land Management, Prineville District, 185 East Fourth Street (Prineville) 97754: 447-4115

John Day Fossil Beds National Monument, 420 West Main Street (John Day) 97845: 575-0721

Kam Wah Chung & Co. Museum, 250 N.W. Canton Street (John Day) 97845: 575-0547

Prairie City Chamber of Commerce, Depot Park and DeWitt Museum 97869: 820-3598

4 ~

Prineville
to Burns

From Prineville take the Post-Paulina Road, which leaves US 26 on the eastern edge of town.

Highlights: *Some of Oregon's most remote mountain and ranching scenery, dramatic lava buttes, colorful aspen and larch, and deer and elk in the forests.*

Prineville is closer to the geographical center of Oregon than any other incorporated town; Post, a store and post office about twenty-five miles southeast on the way to Paulina, is about as close as you can get to the center.

Prineville was founded by Barney Prine who historians tell us built the entire town in a single day: a dwelling house, store, blacksmith shop, hotel, and saloon. Before you think you're reading a Paul Bunyan legend, be aware that his building material was willow logs, and that the stores and home were each ten-by-fourteen feet and that they were all under a single roof.

The area was noted for its vigilantism—the sheriff was 120 miles north in The Dalles—and a particularly nasty range war erupted between sheep and cattle owners with the cattlemen doing most of the shooting. The cattlemen liked to give their groups names like the Ezee Sheep Shooters and the Crook County Sheep Shooters Association. They bragged that in 1905 they killed 10,000 sheep with their saddle guns.

Like the rest of the American West, the days of frequent gunfire have been consigned to history, and the Prineville area is more famous among rock aficionados for the great pickings at several sites on federal land managed by the Bureau of Land Management and Forest Service. The local Chamber of Commerce has brochures and maps. If you are a genuine rockhound, you will be interested in the Annual Prineville Rockhound Show and Pow-Wow held in mid-June. It is attended about equally by rockhounds and prospectors.

A good place to start your education on the area is the A. R. Bowman Museum at 246 North Main Street. It contains a lot of Old West artifacts, such as saddles, harnesses, and clothing. It has an extensive collection for rockhounds, too, including Blue Mountain picture jasper, thunder eggs, and many fossils. The cowboy campfire is an unusual exhibit with the inevitable graniteware coffee pot and a pound of Bull Durham chewing tobacco. A moonshine still, a country store, and a parlor are also on exhibit.

Once you leave Prineville driving southeast toward Paulina and Burns, you make a steady climb out of the valley and onto the edge of the Strawberry Mountains. This is John Ford western-movie scenery with pines, willows, dramatic red and black cliffs, and the stream that named itself: Crooked River. You'll see lots of sagebrush and low-growing, very tough juniper trees. Pioneers used this tree for fence posts. (Reub Long, the most famous citizen of the Oregon desert,

The tiny town of Paulina

claimed it wasn't unusual for a juniper fence post to outlast three or four postholes.)

This region is a continuation of the John Day Country geology and rockhounds routinely find fossils of both flora and fauna from many centuries past. The cliffs overlooking the Crooked River are often seamed by another kind of lava flow, then tilted upward in faults. Some of these seams are so dark against the red stone that they look like coal.

This scenery continues the fifty miles to Paulina, and you have a narrow but paved road from which to enjoy it. This open country with mountains decorating the western horizon and all the colors of the nearby mountains and meadows is one of the most beautiful western landscapes in Oregon.

Surprisingly, Paulina has a highway bypass. The town, named in honor of a renegade Paiute leader, has perhaps twenty buildings, including a community church on a knoll at the edge of town that began its life as a one-room schoolhouse. The highway runs along the side of a hill above the church, the school, the store, and the post office. Services are meager and expensive. The store sells the basic things needed by ranchers in the area, and the only prepared food available is what a Forest Service ranger referred to as "gut-bombs," microwaved burritos and the like.

The Paulina school teaches about two dozen children from kindergarten through eighth grade. After that, they must commute to Prineville each day by bus, a fifty-mile trip, one-way for the lucky ones, but up to seventy-five miles for others who live farther out in the country. A quick calculation shows that the fifty-milers ride the uncomfortable buses 500 miles a week, 18,000 miles a year, 72,000 miles in four years.

Southeast of Paulina the trees dwindle away as the land rises, and thick sagebrush covers the open country. A fork soon appears in the road, offering the option of driving north through the Ochoco National Forest on a dirt road back to State 26 between Mitchell and Dayville. The main route continues on pavement past a sign pointing south to Suplee, which may have been a town at one time but now is nothing more than two ranches.

The road continues climbing for a few miles, then levels off and follows the banks of Pine Creek, which is lined with thick willows that become fiery red in October, giving hunters something to enjoy while waiting for game to come into sight.

No marker shows us where the town of Izee once stood. A highway flag person told me I had passed the schoolhouse, but I didn't see it. I didn't see the road signs, either, and had missed the turn south toward Burns. Had the paving crew not stopped me after about three miles, I would have taken the wrong road to US 395 just south of John Day and Canyon City. I was tempted because it was late in the day, but I wanted to spend the night at Frenchglen, so I turned around and drove back to the intersection near Izee. Two things marked the intersection, neither of which were road signs: a large log building and a sign pointing to a restaurant.

The enormous peeled-log building was the headquarters of a large cattle ranch, the I-Z Cattle Company. A short distance down the road is a small restaurant and bar, called the Bar None, in a former stucco home. It could well be the most remote bar and restaurant in Oregon. When I drove past, the sign said the restaurant was open only three hours a day, from 5:00 P.M. to 8:00 P.M., but the bar is open afternoons and evenings.

From the Bar None it is only a short distance to the Grant-Harney County line, and like so many county boundaries, one county makes the other look bad by ending the pavement at the exact line, then installing a sign marking the division (counties may install boundary signs on every road, but I am only aware of them when one county paves and the other doesn't). Fortunately, the gravel road is in good condition but the directional signs leave something to be desired.

When the pavement begins again, the road to Hines clears an unnamed summit and spread out before you, for miles and miles, is the vastness of the eastern Oregon desert that continues south into California and Nevada and east into Idaho. The road winds along the mountainside, always with views of the desert, and if you are arriving late in the day you will see the lights of Hines and Burns far below you.

The road ends abruptly at US 20 just south of Hines. Turn left, north, to Hines and Burns. If you are going on the next trip described here—through the desert to the Malheur refuge, Frenchglen, and beyond—you can drive south and take a cutoff road east to State 205. However, you will probably be low on gas and will want something to eat and drink, in which case you should drive north to Burns, only two miles away, and follow the directions to Frenchglen.

In the Area

All numbers are within area code 503.

Prineville Chamber of Commerce, 390 North Fairview Street (Prineville) 97754: 447-6304

A. R. Bowman Museum, 246 North Main Street (Prineville) 97754: 447-3715

Ochoco National Forest, Prineville Ranger Station, 2321 East Third Street (Prineville) 97754: 447-3825

Ochoco National Forest, Paulina Ranger District, 6015 Paulina Star Route (Paulina) 97751: 447-3713

Bureau of Land Management, Prineville District Office, 185 East Fourth Street (Prineville) 97754: 447-4115

5 ~

The Heart of the High Desert

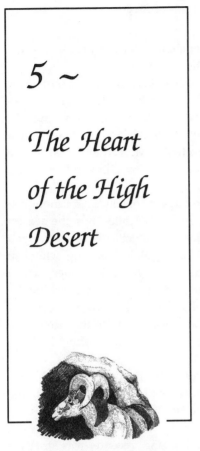

Take State 78 east from Burns two miles and turn south on State 205, which runs due south to Frenchglen to Hart Mountain Antelope Range, Warner Valley, Plush, and on to US 395 just south of Wagontire.

Highlights: *Oregon's high desert, Steens Mountain, Malheur National Wildlife Refuge, Hart Mountain Antelope Range, unusual geological formations at Warner Lakes, Abert Rim, and Lake Abert.*

Oregonians are as proud of their high desert (average elevation is about 4,000 feet) as almost any other part of the state. Its centerpiece is 9,773-foot Steens Mountain, an unusual and remote sentinel that has the Malheur refuge on the west side and on the east the flat-as-a-table Alvord Desert, a moonscape of alkali flats and seasonal brilliant blue lakes.

The Steens Mountain Country is popular with wildlife lovers and bird-watchers, and they come from all over America and a few foreign countries with their binoculars, long camera lenses, and incredible patience to spend almost every daylight hour out in the field. Some camp in their RVs and others stay in the elderly Frenchglen Hotel or the more recent lodging additions around the mountain.

Almost all of the Oregon desert is in Harney County, the largest county in America. It is even larger than nine states— Connecticut, Delaware, Hawaii, Maryland, Massachusetts, New Hampshire, New Jersey, Rhode Island, and Vermont— but has only 7,000-plus residents. More than 3,000 live in Burns, the county seat, and another 2,000 live in Hines, two miles south of Burns.

Harney County has the largest consolidated school district in America; some children live 175 miles from the nearest school. The only practical way these ranch children can attend high school is to have the only public boarding school in America, the coed school at Crane, forty-two miles east of Burns. Boys live on one floor of the dormitory and girls on the other. Teachers must insist that ne'er do the twain meet, and parents, especially those who graduated from the school, are usually too polite to laugh when they hear teachers say it.

This desert trip takes you from Burns to Steens Mountain, then west across the desert to Hart Mountain National Antelope Refuge. It ends at US 395 just south of the two-person town of Wagontire.

Begin at Burns, a town that until recently was strictly a farming and ranching community. Few towns in America are more remote than Burns: 130 miles from Bend, more than 200 miles from Boise, Idaho, 70 miles from John Day, and there's virtually nothing south until Reno. However, as the Steens Mountain area has grown in popularity, Burns has added a few more motels and a scattering of B&Bs, all modestly priced, one or two very good restaurants, and a deli or two.

A good way to appreciate the special problems of the desert is to take a tour of the Bureau of Land Management wild horse corrals near Burns, where you will learn about desert land management, the horse adoption program, and the Kiger mustang herd, which is thought to be the most pure herd of Spanish mustangs in the world.

Burns was named for the Scottish poet, Robert Burns. According to one version, which may or may not be true, a man was sent out on horseback with a list of potential names for the new town to present to ranchers and sheepherders to vote on. The pollster rode out of sight, then went home to bed. A few days later he went back to the new town with the news that his favorite name won the popularity contest.

The Harney County Museum at 18 West D Street is a good place to begin your appreciation for the desert, because it has a large collection of furniture, wagons, a complete pioneer kitchen, and many artifacts from Pete French's ranch. French was the dominant cattleman in the 1870s and 1880s; some say he had the largest cattle operation in America at that time because he controlled more than 800,000 acres of grazing land in Oregon and Nevada, running 80,000 head of cattle and more than 100,000 sheep.

He was as ruthless as he was successful, and he hated homesteaders. In turn, they hated French so much that a story persists that in 1897 sodbusters drew straws to see who would murder him. The winner/loser rode up to French while several of his men were watching, shot him in the head, and rode away. He was able to make his leisurely escape because French's hired hands didn't carry guns.

While the circumstances of the murder remain clouded, what happened during and after the trial is well documented. The homesteaders took up a collection so the accused could hire a good lawyer. He was found innocent by a predominantly sodbuster jury, and he immediately disappeared with the money, leaving his wife and children to fend for themselves.

From downtown Burns take State 78 east, and after two miles turn right (south) on State 205, which runs straight as a laser across the arid Harney Valley to a low ridge that runs north and south, looking like a wall from a distance. After a sudden left turn to climb about 500 feet to the top at Wright's Point, the highway descends quickly into Sunset Valley. Here you will see a few more ranches and irrigated hayfields, and soon cross alkali flats that mark the far reaches of Malheur Lake on the left (east) side of the highway and Harney Lake on the other side.

The lakes have much breadth but little depth, and they rise and fall over periods of several years, presenting a vivid record of fluctuations in the climate. In the mid- and late 1980s, the lake levels rose dramatically, covering hundreds of square miles that were normally barren, and there was concern that the slightly elevated highway that goes between them would be destroyed. Then a series of dry years began in 1990, bringing the levels down again and causing the locals to worry about drought rather than flooding.

If you are driving after dark, do so slowly because you never know when a cow, a deer, or an antelope will suddenly appear in your headlights. After living the good life of the refuge for a few generations, wildlife become more careless than their relatives still out in the wild.

After passing an occasional ranch house, you arrive at the town of Frenchglen, population about ten. Frenchglen was Peter French's headquarters and named for himself and his father-in-law, Dr. Hugh Glenn, who put up the money for French's cattle operation. In spite of its size—and perhaps partly because of it—Frenchglen is one of Oregon's best-known towns and has the state's most remote hotel. The eight-room hotel was built in 1916 by Armour for visiting cattlemen and has been part of the Oregon State Parks' system for a number of years. It is the centerpiece of the town, and visitors who stay in the nearby campground often eat the family-style breakfasts and dinners served in the hotel's combination lobby, sitting room, and dining room.

A bighorn sheep

The refuge headquarters are nearby at the site of Pete French's ranch. Here you can get directions on loop trips around Steens Mountain and through the enormous refuge that is home to more than 300 species of birds, including songbirds, shorebirds, raptors, migratory geese, ducks, and sandhill cranes. In addition, the refuge is home to mule deer, bighorn sheep, numerous small desert animals, plus the usual varieties of snakes.

Steens Mountain lies out in the middle of the desert, something like a beached whale lying on a northeast-southwest axis. The western slopes have been worn down over the years, and its roads have been built along the ridges and valleys left by receding glaciers during the ice ages. The eastern side is completely different. The mountain drops off sheer cliffs down to the flat Alvord Desert. On a clear day you can see Oregon, Idaho, Nevada, and California from the summit.

The mountain's elevation enables it to catch more moisture than the surrounding desert so it has a coating of juniper, sagebrush, and groves of aspen with fields of wildflowers.

You have a choice of loop trips to take through the refuge. One is a twenty-mile trip through Diamond Valley, and the other is a sixty-six-mile odyssey through the refuge and up Steens Mountain to see four enormous U-shaped gorges dredged out by glaciers before dropping back down to the valley floor. Always check at the refuge headquarters before trying the latter trip because the road is subject to closures by snow or flood.

From Frenchglen State 205 heads uphill out of the Blitzen Valley to the broad, open desert. The highway is paved south to the Roaring Springs Ranch, but the turn toward Hart Mountain is seven miles out, and you are faced with nearly forty miles of gravel road that alternates between being very flat and well graded to being riddled with chuckholes and deep ruts. At the end of the last ice age this area was an enormous lake. Allow yourself at least an hour for the forty miles, and don't be surprised if it takes you longer, especially if you have any respect for your vehicle.

The desert is mostly flat here, and sometimes you will think only the curvature of the earth prevents you from seeing the road's end. If you are lucky you will see pronghorns out in the sagebrush, but don't count on it. Although the 275,000-acre Harts Mountain National Antelope Refuge, created in 1936, protects one of the largest herds of antelopes on the continent, they are very shy and skittish and avoid human contact more than the mule deer you will be more likely to see. You may also see cottontails, jackrabbits, and an occasional songbird. Coyotes and bobcats live here, but are seldom found along the road.

You will enter the refuge after the road becomes quite rough. A car can navigate the road safely but watch for deep ruts and rocks that may have been uncovered by erosion.

The headquarters is a collection of buildings near the base of Hart Mountain. The visitors room is always open, and you can pick up brochures, maps, and other information on the refuge. Rockhounding is popular around the mountain, and you are limited to seven pounds per person. Here, as throughout the desert, you can find agate, jasper, petrified wood, thunder eggs, sunstone, and obsidian. Hiking and backpacking are also popular, but a permit must be obtained from the headquarters before making an overnight trip. Some areas are excluded from entry during lambing season for the bighorn sheep.

The road branches at the headquarters, and one arm continues south to Hot Springs Camp, a primitive camping area with a hot springs bathhouse, small lakes, and hiking areas, while the main route heads over Poker Jim Ridge, before dropping 3,000 feet into Warner Valley with its series of shallow lakes of all sizes and other-worldly basaltic topography. Warner Valley has a slight south to north tilt so in wet years the lakes fill from the south and gradually overflow northward until the whole valley looks like inland sea. The Warner Wetlands Area of Critical Environmental Concern is north of Hart Lake, and the Bureau of Land Management is restoring lakes in this area to their aboriginal state. Hot springs are common in the valley; some ranchers have accidentally discovered geysers when they drilled for water and struck pools of hot water.

The dirt road descends a series of zigzags to reach the floor of Warner Valley, then takes a sharp right turn to miss Hart Lake before arriving at the paved county road just north of the very small town of Plush. You can stop here for gas and groceries sold in the same building, but no other services are available.

According to local lore, Plush got its name in an unusual fashion. The bureaucrats working for the postmaster general turned down the first two names submitted. While the residents searched for a suitable name, during a poker game a player said he had a flush. Another player—one version says he was an Indian who had trouble with English, and another says it was a man with a speech impediment—said he was "plush" too. It got such a laugh that the word was submitted to the post office, and it was accepted.

At Plush you can continue south to US 395 and Lakeview. The trip described here goes north on the gravel road another twenty miles to join US 395 a few miles south of Wagontire so the drive will include Abert Rim and Lake Abert.

After driving north from Plush the pavement ends, and the gravel road climbs over a small ridge that is the northern end of the enormous fault, Abert Rim. The road then descends to a long haul across the empty desert to US 395 just north of Abert Rim and Lake Abert. Here you can drive south to Lakeview or north toward Wagontire to catch the highway west to Christmas Valley.

No matter which direction you drive from here, it is worth the additional few minutes to drive south to see Abert Rim and Lake Abert. The rim, called a fault or a scarp, runs several miles along the east side of the highway and is the highest exposed fault in North America. Several of these faults are found in the Oregon desert and are caused by underground pressures against the earth's crust. When the pressures cause a break in the crust, one side of the break is forced upward, creating scarps such as Abert Rim.

Lake Abert, which has no outlet, is on the west side of the highway and in recent years has receded and left a vast white rim around it composed of soda, borax, and the inevitable alkali. Other smaller lakes form in depressions along the base of Abert Rim north to Wagontire, where the fault descends into the flat desert floor.

When you drive north, stop at Wagontire, population two, for gas or a snack. The small restaurant-store-service station has a few stools and tables and an extensive collection of scatological cartoons on the walls and postcards with the same kind of humor. When I stopped for gas and to refill my thermos with cowboy coffee, a military jet fighter, treating the desert as though it is devoid of population, flew over at supersonic speed. The sonic boom shook the building so much that dishes rattled and a display for an oil treatment compound fell off the wall.

In the Area

All numbers are within area code 503.

Harney County Chamber of Commerce, 18 West D Street (Burns) 97720: 573-2636

Bureau of Land Management, Burns District, US 20 West (Burns) 97738: 573-5241

Malheur National Forest, Snow Mountain Ranger District (Hines) 97738: 573-7292

Malheur Wildlife Refuge, PO Box 245 (Princeton) 97721: 493-2612

Hart Mountain National Antelope Refuge, PO Box 111 (Lakeview) 97630: 947-3315

Frenchglen Hotel (Frenchglen) 97736: 493-2825

6 ~

Christmas
Valley

From US 395, nine miles south of Wagontire, drive west on the paved county road to Lost Forest, Fort Rock, and back to Christmas Valley.

Highlights: *Basaltic desert topography, the unusual Lost Forest of Ponderosa pine amid shifting sand dunes, Crack-in-the-Ground, Four Craters, Derrick Cave, Devils Garden, Fort Rock, and failed homesteads.*

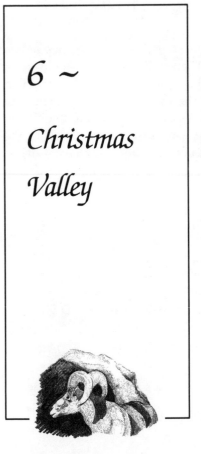

This trip makes a natural continuation of the High Desert trip because it starts between Abert Rim and Wagontire. The paved county road leads about twenty-five miles across the desert that is dotted with juniper and sagebrush. You will see a few ranch houses, most surrounded by windbreaks of various deciduous trees, often Lombardy poplar.

The landscape is rolling, and you'll see the usual clumps of sagebrush and an occasional outcropping of lava. The first real indication that you are in this century, other than the paved road, is the appearance on the horizon of an electrical power substation that makes its presence known by a soldierly line of tall poles running beside the highway before heading off across the desert to wherever large amounts of electrical power go. California, perhaps?

Shortly after these poles become part of the scenery, watch for a sign pointing north, right, to Lost Forest and Sand Dunes. Follow this road until it ends at a T, turn right and soon you will be at the edge of the sand dunes that surround the Lost Forest, which you can see off in the distance. If the road is dry, you can continue on to the edge of the forest. The road is treacherous if it is wet, so it is best to stay out unless you have a four-wheel-drive vehicle. Traffic is light in the dunes and forest, so if you get stranded, you may be there a few hours listening to the wind and the sound of your heartbeat in your ears.

The Lost Forest is called that because it is isolated in the middle of about 16,000 acres of sand dunes, some of which are forty feet high. About 10,000 acres of dunes are open to recreational use, including driving all-terrain vehicles across them. The remaining 6,000 acres form a buffer. The forest is on Bureau of Reclamation land and is protected by a Research Natural Area designation that covers 8,960 acres, which is most of the forest. Entry is restricted to the roads and trails that are posted as open.

Researchers believe the forest is a remnant of a much larger forest that was gradually diminished by volcanic action. Timber is no longer harvested from it, but during the homesteader era, from the 1850s until about 1920, the pine became building materials, fence posts, and firewood. Then the droughts came and drove homesteaders from the land. Studies of Lost Forest tree rings show that the climate was fairly constant for nearly 600 years, then the droughts of 1920 and 1936 struck and dramatically changed the human population patterns not only in Christmas Valley but also in the entire United States.

The forest has several primitive campsites but be aware that there is no water, that the sand blows easily, and that walking is very difficult. For most visitors a look at the forest from the sand dunes is enough before turning around and heading toward Christmas Valley. Retrace your route back to the T, return to the highway, and go another seven miles toward Christmas Valley until you come to another intersection that leads you on a rough road to Four Craters Wilderness Study Area. It is a good idea to drive on to Christmas Valley to ask for a map or directions, then drive back to the intersection.

The Four Craters refers to a cluster of four cinder cones. Nearby is Crack-in-the-Ground, a two-mile-long crack in the lava that is fifty feet deep in places. Geologists believe the crack was formed about 1,000 years ago when a basalt layer collapsed during eruptions of the nearby cinder cones. When you walk through some of the crack on developed trails, note how perfectly the parts would fit if the walls moved back together.

Some of the cinder cones here look like meteor-impact areas, but geologists are convinced that they were caused by volcanic action, subterranean explosions that blew holes out of the ground and shot lava into the air. Over the centuries erosion gradually smoothed the holes' sides and they became more round.

If you would like to have a picnic, try stopping at the Green Mountain lookout and camping area near the four craters. You are welcome to visit the lookout unless fire operations are in progress. Be warned that neither the camping area nor the lookout have water or restrooms.

Your next stop on this dirt road will be the Squaw Ridge Lava Flow Wilderness Study Area, which has been protected for its excellent collection of *aa* lava, the kind that forms into blocks of basalt as opposed to the ropelike *pahoehoe* lava, which is very smooth and looks almost like chocolate cake batter.

About six miles west of Squaw Ridge is the Devils Garden Wilderness Study Area, where lava flows surrounded but didn't quite cover a patch of ground. The uncovered patch of ground is of interest to researchers studying plant life and soil composition before the enormous lava flows. On the northern end of Devils Garden is Derrick Cave, a quarter-mile-long lava tube that has served both as a study area for geologists and a bomb shelter for nervous civil-defense officials. During the early stages of World War II, when the Japanese dropped some incendiary bombs on the Oregon coast, civil-defense officials turned the lava tube into a bomb shelter for local citizens. When the Cuban missile crisis occurred a decade later and Americans were worried about atomic or hydrogen warfare, Lake County's Search and Rescue Unit built a steel gate across the entrance and stored C-rations and jerrycans of water.

You can walk back into the tube, but wear sturdy shoes to protect your feet from the sharp rocks and take flashlights with strong batteries.

The very small town of Fort Rock is about fourteen miles away. It has virtually no visitor facilities, but you can stop at the store for drinks and picnic supplies. On the edge of town is the Homestead Village Museum, a collection of buildings including a church, two homes, a log cabin, and a doctor's office.

In 1938, in a small cave two miles from Fort Rock, an archaeology professor found a cache of seventy-five sandals made of sagebrush bark that were carbon-dated at more than 9,000 years old.

A short distance north on a county road is the volcanic formation and state park of the same name. Fort Rock was

A pronghorn antelope at Fort Rock

formed by explosive volcanic eruptions beneath a lake, and the walls were formed when the lava fell back down and cooled. Geologists have two versions of how it got its horse-shoe shape: One is that lava breached one side; the other is that waves from the vast lake that covered the area broke down the wall. Whatever caused it left the structure looking like part of a sports stadium, which is what the former owner, Reub Long, jokingly said he would build in it. Instead, he and his sister donated it as a state park. He once told a visitor that he bought Fort Rock so he could climb to a favorite spot on the rim and sit in the silence and enjoy the end of a day. Nearby are several remnants of the homesteader years: abandoned cabins and windmills and bits and pieces of machinery.

This is an appropriate time to pay homage to the late R. A. "Reub" Long, who was one of Oregon's most beloved personalities. Reub lived in the Fort Rock area most of his life and was one of the desert's most powerful ranchers. However, Long used his power for the good of all his neighbors, and, if he were still among us, he probably would be irritated to hear someone use the word *power* and his name in the same sentence.

Mostly, though, Long was a philosopher and folklorist. He collected desert wit and wisdom, and one of his friends, a county extension agent named E. R. Jackman, suggested that they collaborate on a book. It was called *The Oregon Desert* and was published by The Caxton Printers in Caldwell, Idaho, in 1967. It was accepted by nearly everyone as an instant classic and has been selling steadily ever since.

Jackman was the historian and naturalist in the book, and almost a secretary to Long. He wrote down what Long told him: tall tales, jokes, one-liners, and folk wisdom. Long liked to gently pull the reader's leg. For example, he said the only thing he ever did that was unique was perform a Caesarean on a mama porcupine. Typically, he didn't explain the circumstances.

Here is a sampling of the wisdom he passed along to readers:

> The older I get, the better I used to be.
>
> As a man rises in the world, his luxuries of yesterday become today's necessities.
>
> Conduct yourself in such a manner that you are in good company when you are alone.

Some politicians remind me of a man I saw sneaking down through the brush riding a clumsy old big-footed white mare with a bell on.

The reason I've been able to produce some fast horses is that, where I graze them, they have to feed at thirty miles an hour to get enough to eat.

To complete the Christmas Valley loop, drive west from Fort Rock to State 31 and take it southeast past Silver Lake to the Christmas Valley road. The town of Christmas Valley, originally built as a retirement town, has gas, food, and lodging. From here you can go back to State 31, which leads northwest to La Pine and Bend and southeast to Lakeview. An alternative is to take a county road just west of Silver Lake through national forest land to US 97 about forty miles north of Klamath Falls.

In the Area

All numbers are within area code 503.

Bureau of Land Management, Lakeview Resource Area, PO Box 151 (Lakeview) 97630: 947-2177

Desert Inn (Christmas Valley) 97630: 576-2262

Fort Rock Valley Historical Society: 576-2327

7 ~

The Other

Route 66

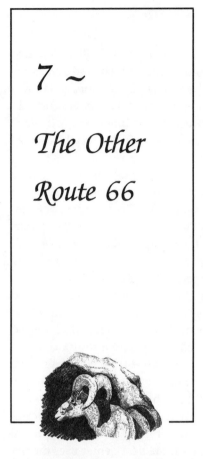

From Klamath Falls go south on US 97 to intersection with State 66. Follow it across the Cascades until it intersects with I-5 at Ashland.

Highlights: *Geothermal power system and museums of Klamath Falls, mountain scenery along part of the old Oregon Trail, country inns, old-growth Douglas fir and sugar pine, panoramic views of the Siskiyou Mountains, and the cultural life of Ashland.*

By the time you reach Klamath Falls (called K Falls here), you are near the California border and almost out of the Cascade Range. The mountains are well worn down by now and the last tall peak you'll see in Oregon is 9,495-foot Mount McLoughlin, which makes a striking backdrop for Upper Klamath Lake, just north of town. The Cascades meander on into California and disappear just south of Mount Lassen, the last of the Cascade volcanoes.

This makes State 66 between Klamath Falls and Ashland less challenging than some of the other mountain roads—more of a country drive than a trek—but one of the prettiest

47

routes in southern Oregon. The highway is well maintained and a scattering of country inns, a guest ranch, and occasional motels are along the way. The area is popular for Ashlanders as well as Klamath Falls residents, and several weekend cabins stand beside mountain streams. Old-timers know it as the Green Springs Road as well as State 66. It also has the distinction of being the state's most crooked cross-Cascades route.

Before striking out on the highway, you will probably want to spend some time driving and walking around Klamath Falls with its several historic buildings. The Chamber of Commerce has printed a brochure to guide you on a walking tour. It is almost surrounded by the two-part Klamath Lake, and much of the lake has been given over to wildlife refuges. Few cities this size have wildlife refuges literally at their door.

Klamath Falls has a long history of geothermal power and is said to be the largest geographical area in America to use this form of energy. This obviously makes the city a respected leader in the use of geothermal energy and a source of information for other potential users. More than 500 wells have been drilled in the immediate area to use the underground hot water. The Oregon Institute of Technology on the north end of town uses the hot water year-round; in the summer, water is used for cooling and in the winter for snow and ice removal on the sidewalks. The Merle West Medical Center uses the hot water for laundry, and the government uses it to heat the jail and regional state offices. Many homes have tapped into this energy source and in some residential areas you will see steam rising from vents that are used as safety valves.

With so many people using the heated water, the local government has a program encouraging people to either replace any water taken out of the ground, or simply to use the hot water to heat water without removing it from the ground and lowering the water table.

The geothermal story is explained in exhibits in the Klamath County Museum, along with an extensive natural history collection that reflects the area's importance to the Pacific Flyway, the route taken by migratory waterfowl. The museum also has a notable collection of artifacts from the Modoc Indians who lived in the area and relics from the shameful Modoc war of 1872–73.

Klamath Falls' best-known art and history repository is the Favell Museum, housing several large private collections of Indian artifacts, particularly those of the Favell family, and more than 60,000 mounted arrowheads. Its western art collection is considered one of the best in the world with paintings, sculpture, and pottery by nearly all major living and many dead western artists.

State 66 has been designated a historic highway by the state because it is along the trail blazed by Jesse and Lindsay Applegate during the migration over the Oregon Trail. Known as the Applegate Cutoff, the route caused tremendous hardship for families migrating to the Willamette Valley, and some never got over their hatred of the Applegates for leading them on it.

Supposedly a shortcut to the Willamette Valley, this alternate route began at American Falls, Idaho, and swung south into the deserts of Nevada and California. It then veered north into Oregon and after crossing the Cascades, it followed the same route as I-5. The route came into being because one of Applegate's sons had drowned when a raft flipped over in the Columbia River on an earlier trip. He and his two brothers, Charles and Lindsay, were determined to find a better route.

The route has had several names. After a period as the Applegate Cutoff, it became the Southern Oregon Wagon Road when a roadway was cleared through the mountains between 1868 and 1873. It later became the Green Springs Highway when the state declared it a state highway in 1917.

This trip begins at the intersection of State 66 with US 97 on the south end of Klamath Falls and ends sixty miles later when it reaches I-5 just outside Ashland. These sixty miles are among the most beautiful you will find in Oregon.

The first few miles are along the Klamath River valley with low ridges to the south and lots of wooden fences, corrals, neat homes, old barns, horse trailers, and stacks of baled hay. Late in the afternoon you will sometimes see people out riding horses.

The last town of any size is Keno, named for a pioneer's bird dog, about ten miles out of Klamath Falls on the northern edge of the Lower Klamath National Wildlife Area. This is your last chance to stock up on picnic supplies and gas.

Much of the timber along the highway is still old-growth, and on clear mornings and afternoons the sun will flicker through hypnotically as you drive past Douglas fir, sugar pine, dogwood, and various kinds of underbrush.

A typical Oregon woodland scene

While the two mountain passes aren't very high—the Hayden Mountain Summit and Parker Mountain Summit are under 5,000 feet, an elevation gain of less than 1,000 feet from Klamath Falls—the mountains are often quite steep. Consequently, the highway has many curves that will keep your speed down. It is just as well; if you drive white-knuckled through these mountains, you will miss the beauty around you.

If you consider that the wagon trains going through here had to crawl through the timber as well as ford the rocky streams and climb the mountains, it is easy to see why the overlanders were upset with their leaders. Even though the Applegates thought they were doing a good deed, the trip was terrible. One woman wrote later that she lost everything but the horse she was riding and the clothes on her back, and said that only one wagon came through without breaking. She also wrote that the canyons were strewn with dead cattle, provisions, broken wagons, beds, and clothing as the immigrants tried to get to the Willamette Valley before the winter snows. The state has placed markers at known ferry points and places where the pioneers forded streams.

Once you reach the crest of the Cascades and descend toward Ashland, the number of deciduous trees increases, particularly live oak, and the evergreen timber thins. More homes begin appearing in the Pinehurst area, some of which are summer homes for Ashland residents. The Pinehurst Inn overlooking a creek has meals and rooms. It is part of the nearby Box R ranch, which is a working ranch that also takes in guests.

Tubb Springs State Park is a small picnic wayside with restrooms, and nearby is the Cold Springs Inn that offers food and lodging.

The last six or eight miles on the road to Ashland are very crooked. The highway presents an almost endless number of curves, but there's also an occasional turnout so you can stop to relax, let the brakes cool, and enjoy the scenery of khaki-colored rolling hills dotted with oak trees. The landscape on this side of the Cascades looks much like the Sonoma or Napa areas of California. Numerous homes have been built in the hills, and you can expect more traffic in the mornings and evenings. State 66 ends at the intersection with I-5 on the edge of Ashland.

This is one of those small towns with a big reputation. World-class theater, the Oregon Shakespeare Festival, has been going since 1935. A local college teacher named Angus Bowmer talked the merchants, in the midst of the Great Depression, into building an Elizabethan stage to celebrate the Fourth of July with two of Shakespeare's plays. Taking no chances on the box office, the locals added two boxing matches at intermissions.

To nearly everyone's surprise, Shakespeare caught on and has had a growing following ever since. The Bard has done so well that you'll have to rely on ESPN for boxing. The festival runs from February through October with eleven plays by Shakespeare and a sampling of other playwrights, including contemporary ones. The flimsy stage of 1935 has had three sturdy replacements.

Ashland also has the Oregon Cabaret Theater for popular musicals, the Rogue Valley Symphony for classical concerts, an opera company, children's theater, and other similar offerings. The town hosts a large number of other festivals and events, and of course has a large number of restaurants and delis, hotels, motels, bed and breakfasts, and country inns.

After Shakespeare, Ashland is most proud of its 100-acre Lithia Park, which has been designated a National Historic Place. It is named for the mineral springs in the park that contain a healthy dose of lithium. Although the water is both effervescent and sulfurous, many people drink it from the fountains throughout the park and insist it is good for them.

In the Area

All numbers are within area code 503.

Klamath County Department of Tourism, PO Box 1867
(Klamath Falls) 97601: 884-0666 or (800) 445-6728

Favell Museum, 125 West Main Street (Klamath Falls) 97601:
882-9996

Pinehurst Inn, 17250 State 66 (Ashland) 97520: 488-1002

Green Springs Box R Ranch, 16799 State 66 (Ashland) 97520:
482-1873

Ashland Chamber of Commerce, 110 East Main Street
(Ashland) 97520: 482-3486

Southern Oregon Reservation Center, PO Box 477
(Ashland) 97520: 488-1011 or (800) 547-8052

8 ~

The Applegate Valley

From Medford take State 238 to Jacksonville to Ruch, turn left (south) on Applegate Road to Applegate Lake, looping back on Thompson Creek Road to State 238 again at Applegate. Follow State 238 to Grants Pass or turn left on South Side Road along the Applegate River to US 199 and take it east to Grants Pass or south to Oregon Caves and California.

Highlights: *Historic Jacksonville, a beautiful and secluded river valley, orchards, wineries, a covered bridge, lake, and the only known Sasquatch trap.*

As indicated in the State 66 trip, Applegate is one of the most important names in Oregon, especially the southern part of the state. Of the three brothers—Lindsay, Charles, and Jesse—history remembers Jesse the most. He became the dominant name in the family, whether he wanted it that way or not, and was southern Oregon's patriarch.

After the Applegates settled in the Oregon Territory, Jesse wrote a small book entitled *A Day with the Cow Column* in 1843, a description of a single day during the great migration across the continent. Cinematic in its treatment of the experience, the book is still the most vivid of all the descriptions of life on the trail. Here is the first paragraph of the book:

> It is 4 o'clock A.M. The sentinels on duty have discharged their rifles—the signals that the hours of sleep are over. Every wagon and tent is pouring forth its night tenants. The slow-kindling smokes begin largely to rise and float away on the morning air. Sixty men start from the corral—spreading as they make their way through the vast herd of cattle and horses that forms a semicircle around the encampment, the most distant perhaps two miles away.

President Lincoln offered him the job of territorial governor, which he declined. Nearly everyone who came to Oregon in those pioneer years called on Jesse Applegate and spoke of his intelligence and graciousness. Only one sketch of Jesse survives; he was a homely man and very self-conscious about it and refused to sit for portraits, painted or photographed. The lone surviving portrait is a sketch drawn by a nephew several years after Jesse died.

With all this said about Jesse Applegate, he didn't even live in the Applegate Valley. He made his home some distance north in the Yoncalla area. Early settlers honored his brother Lindsay by naming the small river and its valley in his honor (and for no better reason than Lindsay passed through enroute to California during the gold rush of 1849). The Applegate name is still very important in Oregon and each year the descendants hold a reunion.

This trip follows State 238 down the Applegate River through the Applegate Valley past the community of Applegate with a side trip to Applegate Lake. The route also connects two of the region's largest towns—Grants Pass and

Medford—and goes through Jacksonville, one of Oregon's best preserved and most authentic historic towns.

Medford, built on the bank of Bear Creek ten miles before it empties into the Rogue River, has a rich agricultural industry with an emphasis on fruit. If you visit in the spring, you will be treated to a dazzling display of blossoms on the pear, apple, peach, plum, and almond trees, plus the flowers that decorate nearly every home and many downtown businesses.

Because the climate is mild and the valley so beautiful, the area has become a mecca for retired couples. Medford was established during Jacksonville's gold-rush days when the railroad came through. Now the town is probably best known for Harry & David's, the mail-order fruit and flower company that provides many jobs year-round and hires hundreds more during the winter holiday season.

Jacksonville is five miles down a highway lined with orchards and attractive homes. The small town with false-front buildings, many made of brick and stone, is a remnant of a short-lived stampede in 1852, when two prospectors found gold on Jackson Creek. A town, Table Rock City, was built immediately but soon became known as Jacksonville. Enough gold was found to finance some impressive Carpenter-Gothic homes, many of which still stand. It was the county seat and in 1883 taxpayers built a striking courthouse that stood sixty feet tall with fourteen-inch-thick walls. It still stands and houses the museum.

Eventually the county seat was moved to the larger and more conveniently located Medford. When the Great Depression struck in the 1930s, interest in gold grew and residents of Jacksonville began burrowing in their backyards and empty lots, creating a mass of tunnels, almost none of which were mapped. Over the years this has led to occasional cave-ins at unexpected places; some family cars have been victims of these mishaps, but in 1992 the Chamber of Commerce

Jeremiah Nunan House in Jacksonville

assured potential visitors that during the past eight years, nobody had lost a car in this fashion.

Jacksonville's best-known event is the Britt Festivals, a summer-long series of concerts of classical, popular, jazz, ethnic, and country music. The event is named in honor of Peter Britt, an early resident who was a pioneer vineyard owner and also a superb photographer who was the first to document the beauty of Crater Lake.

The entire town of Jacksonville has been designated a National Historic District. Only seven other towns in America have earned that distinction. In spite of its fame, Jacksonville has remained very small, and your arrival and departure can be accomplished almost simultaneously, so find a place to park as soon as you can and have a look around. Among the town's most interesting offerings, in addition to the Britt Festival, is the Jacksonville Courthouse Museum, where Peter Britt's cameras and photo collection are exhibited, the Jacksonville Doll Museum, and a tour of the town's cemetery.

Lovers of Carpenter-Gothic homes will enjoy a tour of the Jeremiah Nunan House. It is known as the Catalog House because its owner ordered it from the George F. Barber Cottage Souvenir Catalog in 1892 as a Christmas gift for his wife. It arrived from Knoxville in fourteen boxcars, and when it was completed six months later the whole thing had cost Nunan $7,800.

State 238 follows a narrow, snug valley down to the community of Ruch, where the Applegate River and Little Applegate River merge. This valley is pretty year-round with its beautiful homes, wood smoke coming from chimneys, trees almost forming a canopy over the highway, and rustic signs offering manure for sale. Watch for the Log Town Cemetery on the south side of the highway with graves dating back to the first settlers. A yellow rose bush brought from Missouri in 1851 and planted at one grave site still blooms each year.

To add a loop trip to your drive, take Applegate Road, which turns left (south) here and follows the river for about ten miles to Applegate Lake behind a dam built by the Army Corps of Engineers. About halfway down you will cross the river on (or through) the McKee covered bridge. The 120-foot-long bridge is one of the longest in Oregon. It was built in 1917, which also makes it one of Oregon's oldest; only the Drift Creek Bridge near Lincoln City, built in 1914, predates it. You'll find a picnic area beside the bridge with a popular swimming hole nearby.

Applegate Lake is small with only an eighteen-mile shoreline, but it has a dozen picnic and campsites along the shore, places to swim and fish. For an interesting hike, ask for directions to the Gin Lin Trail, which leads to an area Chinese miners worked during the gold-rush years of the past century.

You can retrace your route back to Ruch or continue on the loop trip. The road becomes the Thompson Creek Road and joins State 238 at the town of Applegate.

Applegate is very small but has that destination-town look with a trendy restaurant along the river. While you're there, you might want to inquire about what may be the only Bigfoot, or Sasquatch, trap in existence.

In 1974, when stories of Sasquatch sightings were frequent, an organization called North American Wildlife Research was determined to capture a Sasquatch alive. They picked what they thought was a gathering place on the Collins Mountain Trail for the mythical creatures, and there they built a ten-foot-square trap of two-by-twelve lumber with a door of heavy metal grating in a steel frame. Assuming the creatures were enormously strong, they anchored it with telephone poles. They baited it with dead rabbits for awhile, but gave up and abandoned the trap.

The unused trap still stands and has since become quite an attraction. In 1992 the Forest Service announced it would erect an interpretive sign. For directions, ask in Applegate or the Rogue River National Forest in Medford.

From Applegate to Grants Pass, the highway wends its way between well-advertised plant nurseries ("You have just past [sic] Applegate Gardens," stated one sign), dairy farms, and produce stands offering potatoes and other vegetables, flowers, and bulbs.

The highway brings you into Grants Pass quite suddenly. It is a small town strung out along the Rogue River with old US 99 running along the west side of the Rogue and I-5 on the north side. The town began as a rest stop on the stage line from California and got its name when a messenger told a group of road builders that General Ulysses Grant had won the battle of Vicksburg. They called it Grant at first, but the post office told them Oregon already had a settlement named for the general, so Pass was added.

The town is perhaps best known as the jumping-off place for boating and fishing trips on the Rogue River and for the Oregon Caves National Monument. The open-air Grower's Market on First Street between Sixth and Seventh avenues is a popular spot for residents and visitors.

If you're driving south and in no particular hurry, take the US 99 route along the west side of the Rogue River for the riverfront scenery.

In the Area

All numbers are within area code 503.

Medford Chamber of Commerce, 305 South Central Street (Medford) 97501: 772-5194

Rogue River National Forest, 333 West 8th Street (Medford) 97501: 776-3585

Historic Jacksonville Chamber of Commerce, PO Box 33 (Jacksonville) 97530: 899-8118

Britt Festival, PO Box 1124 (Medford) 97501: (800) 882-7488

The Jeremiah Nunan House, 635 North Oregon Street (Jacksonville) 97530: 899-1890

9 ~

The

Rogue

River

From I-5 take the Merlin exit (61) four miles north of Grants Pass to Merlin and Galice and follow the road over the Coast Range to Wedderburn. The route is marked 34-8-36 on BLM-managed land but changes to Road 23 when it goes through Forest Service land.

Highlights: *The famous Rogue River with its wilderness areas, steep canyons, rapids, deer, river-front parks, a very crooked road through dark forest, scenic over-looks, the forty-mile Rogue River Hiking Trail, and jetboat or in-flatable trips.*

This trip takes you along most of one of the state's most famous rivers, from the Grants Pass area through the Coast Range and on westward until the Rogue River empties into the Pacific Ocean at Wedderburn.

Mention the Rogue River and images of a wild and beautiful river come to mind, along with several famous names. Zane Grey loved the Rogue like no other river and wrote a novel about it, *Rogue River Feud.* Clark Gable and Gary Cooper loved to visit and fish the river, as have many of the rich and famous. It has also been the setting for numerous movies, including the John Wayne and Katharine Hepburn action-comedy *Rooster Cogburn.*

The drive over the Coast Range isn't dangerous—most of the roads are paved and those that aren't are well maintained—but it is a slow trip because the roads are steep and crooked in many places. Also, you will probably want to stop frequently to enjoy the river and mountain scenery. So pack a picnic hamper, fill your thermos, and plan on spending a full day on the road. If you are thinking of stopping along the way for a float trip or a ride in a jetboat, you may want to make it an overnight trip. Several resorts and inns operate on both sides of the mountains.

The whole trip is nearly 100 miles and shouldn't be attempted in the winter when snow and heavy rains hit; in fact the road is often closed during periods of heavy snowfall.

The best-known portion is along the eighty-four-mile stretch that is part of the Wild and Scenic Rivers designation. The designation covers roughly one-quarter mile on either side of the river, beginning at the mouth of the Applegate River near Grants Pass and continuing all the way to the river's estuary on the coast at Wedderburn.

The first fifteen miles of this trip have some recreational and residential developments, a good paved road along a pretty valley with horses in pastures and trees with moss beards hanging from branches. On some mornings a ribbon of fog follows the river through the valley. The timber here, mostly in the Siskiyou National Forest, is quite dense, and the landscape gets very rugged as the valley tips upward and becomes mountains.

You can expect to see deer grazing on lawns along the river, and an abundance of plump gray squirrels on fence posts, in trees, and scurrying back and forth across the road.

You'll also find several well-maintained parks along the lower elevations, including Hog Creek Landing, which has a public boat ramp. Here outfitters launch inflatables and

An incense cedar tree

kayaks for a fourteen-mile trip down to Grave Creek. You can go with a group or rent a kayak or inflatable for a do-it-your-self trip.

You can also make arrangements to have your car shuttled ahead if you're floating the river or hiking all or part of the forty-mile Rogue River Hiking Trail. This trail begins at the Grave Creek landing and the small town of Illahe. Most hikers plan on five days for the trip. Check with either the Forest Service or Bureau of Land Management offices given in the listings at the end of the chapter for more information.

Indian Mary Park is a remnant of what is believed to be the smallest Indian reservation ever granted by the government. Indian Mary's father, Umpqua Joe, saved a group of white settlers from a massacre, and in 1894 this speck of a reservation was given to Mary in gratitude. She operated a ferry at the site for many years. After her death the county took over its management and turned it into a popular spot for campers and boaters.

The last stop for food or gas is at Galice, a small cluster of buildings along the river where you'll probably see deer grazing in yards, calm as cattle. Here you can also rent boats, arrange for shuttle service, and stay overnight.

Just west of Galice the river begins developing rapids and all along here you will see homes situated among the trees, boat-launching sites, and small parks. Soon after passing the county-operated Alameda Bar Park, the road climbs 500 feet above the river and crosses the Hellgate Bridge. At the west end of the bridge is a fork in the road. The right fork is north on the BLM's Marial National Scenic Byway, which follows the Rogue a short distance to Grave Creek, then loops north around the river and comes back to it again on the north shore at Marial.

Each riffle and rapid on the Rogue has a name, and as with most rivers, they commemorate an event or a person, sometimes reflecting a macabre sense of humor: Crash your boat into a rock and the rock is named in your honor. Coal Riffle got its name when a scow loaded with coal was wrecked there, and Wake Up Riley Riffle was named when the partner of a prospector named Judge Riley found some gold near camp and dashed into camp shouting, "Wake up Riley, we've struck it rich!" Unfortunately, Riley didn't wake up, having died in his sleep.

The main route, which this trip follows, takes the left turn at Hellgate Bridge and begins climbing immediately along the face of the canyon over Hellgate Creek. At the summit, a turnout has a spectacular view of the countryside.

For the next fifty or sixty miles you will be driving through the high country and away from the Rogue River. The road becomes gravel and remains crooked most of the time. The forest becomes more coastal in character with lots of salal, other underbrush, and Douglas fir, sometimes with roots protruding out of banks almost overhead.

Usually you will have the road to yourself, although you should be especially careful on the very crooked portions in case you meet a car, or even a motor home, coming over from the coast. After leaving Hellgate you won't find developed picnic sites, but you'll find many good places to turn off for a rest or a snack.

The route is well marked and for the most part the signs will point the way to the coast. If there's ever any doubt, remember that you need to stay on the road marked either 34-8-36 or simply Road 23. Since the route was developed for federal employees and loggers, you'll find some sections paved and well tended and other sections quite rough, depending on how the section is used.

You'll reach pavement again a short distance east of Agness, and in autumn leaves and larch needles will virtually cover the roadway, making it very slick when wet. Edges of the pavement are bright green with moss. You'll know you're back in civilization again when the pavement is suddenly marked with a center line and lines along the edges. After groping your way through the forest and over the mountains, those lines will be as welcome as a soda machine in Death Valley.

The rest of the drive from Agness on down to Wedder-burn is almost anticlimactic, although very pretty. You might see an occasional jetboat running up the river. The most famous one is the mail boat that takes passengers on its run up to Agness. This service began in 1895 when Elijah Price and his son, Nobel, won the contract to deliver mail. They poled and rowed their boat the forty miles to Agness and Illahe. No passengers were taken.

The river empties into the Pacific just below the ornate bridge on US 101. Gold Beach is to the south, and Wedder-burn is across the bridge to the north.

In the Area

All numbers are within area code 503.

Rogue River National Forest, 333 West 8th Street (Medford) 97501: 776-3585

Bureau of Land Management, 3040 Biddle Road(Medford) 97504: 776-2234

Hellgate Excursions, 953 S.E. 7th Street (Grants Pass) 97526: (800) 648-4874 or 479-7204

Gold Beach Chamber of Commerce, 1225 South Ellensburg Street (Gold Beach) 97444: 247-7526 or (800) 525-2334

10 ~

Not So

Remote

From Bandon on US 101, take State 42 to Coquille, past the two-building town of Remote, over the Coast Range down to the Lookingglass Valley and the I-5 corridor at Roseburg.

Highlights: *The beautiful coast-line at Bandon and the Coquille River estuary, the Coquille River valley, Coquille and Myrtle Point, a covered bridge, and the highway winding along the Coquille River and over the Coast Range into Camas Valley.*

The Oregon coast is connected to the Willamette Valley and the southern part of the I-5 corridor by several two-lane high-ways across the Coast Range, all considerably faster routes than the one I used to get from Grants Pass to the coast at Wedderburn. There are nearly a dozen of these east-west routes, and the major ones are Bandon to Roseburg (de-scribed here); Reedsport to Sutherlin and Curtin; Florence to Eugene and Junction City; Waldport to Corvallis; Newport to Corvallis; Lincoln City to Salem and Portland; Tillamook to Portland; Seaside-Cannon Beach to Portland; and Astoria to Portland.

These routes are almost interchangeable for the casual visitor because they traverse similar terrain by following a river valley back into the mountains and dense forest, rising over a low pass, and then descending into rich agricultural valleys. The Bandon to Roseburg route is typical.

Meteorologists and geologists will undoubtedly say I'm oversimplifying a complex phenomenon when I state that the climate and scenery along the Oregon coast changes south of Coos Bay. Be that as it may, that's the way it seems to me. The coastline doesn't seem to be quite as damp, and the forest doesn't come right down to the beach. The coast begins looking more like the northern California coastline with thinning pine forests and a scattering of live oak trees. To a lesser extent it looks like some coastlines I've seen in Scotland's Shetland and Orkney islands. However, drive only a few miles inland and you'll soon see the familiar thick evergreen timber with moss hanging like Christmas ornaments.

As you drive south on US 101, it swings inland to avoid Coos Bay and doesn't return to the coastline again until Bandon, where it retreats inland again and doesn't reveal the coast until Port Orford. This first town, Bandon, is worth the wait and is one of my favorites because it is less gaudy than many coastal towns. (Is it my imagination or do some coastal towns north of Coos Bay seem to have so little confidence in their natural setting that the residents feel they need glitter to get attention?)

Bandon has what I think is the most beautiful setting of them all. Its collection of sea stacks and pinnacles along the shore is dramatic any time of the day, but particularly in the evening when the low sun hits the rocks. Some are so flat on top that they could almost be petrified stumps left behind by a very tall logger. The Coquille River enters the ocean on the north edge of town. The pleasant park on the river's north side has good views of the town, the lighthouse, and the coast. Coquille means "shell" in French, and received its

The Coquille River light tower at Bandon

name when a wandering Frenchman noted the piles of shells left by Native Americans around the river mouth.

Bandon, sometimes referred to as Bandon-by-the-Sea, has a tragic history of fires. It burned in 1914 and again in 1936. The second fire was the worst and was caused by the proliferation of gorse, a shrub imported from Ireland by the cofounder of Bandon, George Bennett, who was also known as Lord Bennett. Feeling a bit homesick, he wrote home to Ireland for some seeds so he could plant a hedge of the spiky plant that looks something like scotch broom. Gorse thrived in the Bandon climate and spread so rapidly that it went completely out of control. It grew in the dense forest where other shrubs and brush would not and crowded out less aggressive plants until Bandon sometimes looked like an island in a sea of gorse.

On September 26, 1936, the weather was unusually dry and the gorse caught fire from cinders blown from slash fires all around the town. Gorse is so oily and bursts into flame so easily that to some residents it seemed that the plant almost ignited itself from spontaneous combustion. The small fire department spent the day putting out an epidemic of fires. Late that evening the people of Bandon thought they heard an explosion, but it was actually a monstrous fire starting in a clump of gorse. The fire fighters were helpless. They called out everyone who could help fight the fire and emptied the movie theater for helpers. At eleven that night the fire department and the Coast Guard decided to give up and evacuate the town. They had waited almost too long, and residents literally had to flee for their lives. On September 26, Bandon had nearly 500 structures. On September 27, only sixteen remained standing.

These few buildings constitute the core of Old Town, an area of gift shops and antique stores. Here, as nearly everywhere along the coast, you can buy all manner of gift items made of myrtlewood, an extremely slow-growing tree in the Coast Mountains that is a favorite among woodworkers because of its color and grain. After half a century of misinformation, the truth is finally winning the battle against signs and brochures that lead us to believe that this myrtle tree grows only along the Oregon coast and in the Holy Land of the Middle East. That's not true; they are not the same species.

After leaving the coast at Bandon, State 42 follows the edge of the narrow Coquille River Valley rather than tramping across the good bottomland that has been divided into many small farms and dairies. Sometimes the old elm and maple trees beside the road form a canopy overhead. You'll pass myrtlewood factories with enormous root burls stacked outside waiting to be rendered into wall hangings, clock mounts, salad bowls, salt and pepper shakers, and hundreds of other uses. The highway along here is also notable for the high stacks of firewood you'll see outside homes at the beginning of winter.

Coquille is the first town of any size on this route and is the seat of Coos County rather than the larger and more familiar Coos Bay over on the coast. Coquille was built at the head of steamboat navigation on its namesake river, and several of its original Victorian mansions have survived the threat of fires and mildew.

The highway follows the Coquille River on a southerly course to Myrtle Point, which calls itself the "Small Town with the Big Spirit." Myrtle Point has the unusual Coos County Logging Museum housed in a former church, built in 1910, and modeled after the Mormon Tabernacle in Salt Lake City. As its name indicates, myrtlewood trees grow in abundance in the area, and if you want to see more of the timber, try the small Coquille Myrtle Grove State Park, eleven miles south of town on a secondary road.

It is only a short distance from Myrtle Point to the Sandy Creek covered bridge, just a few yards off the highway on the north side. The sixty-foot-long bridge, no longer in service, was built in 1921. A small park with a picnic area and rest-room facilities adjoins the bridge.

Across the highway is the three-building (home, barn, and the multipurpose store–post office–gas pump) town of Remote. It is no longer remote, with the highway traffic roaring past a few feet away, but in the pioneer years when transportation consisted of rowing and poling boats up the Coquille River, Remote was well named.

The rest of the drive is through a beautiful forest on a good highway that follows the twists and turns of the river valley up to the low (1,472 feet) Camas Pass before dropping down into the Camas Valley and I-5. The area got its name from the camas plant that was a dietary staple for Native Americans. Camas has a blue flower, and when the first settlers arrived, they were unfamiliar with it and mistook the valley with a blue floor for a vast lake. The plant's bulb is quite starchy, and the Native Americans cooked them by digging a pit and building a fire in it to heat stones. The bulbs were placed on the stones, and everything was covered with dirt. The settlers preferred to mash the roots into a pulp and bake camas pies.

In the Area

All numbers are within area code 503.

Bandon Chamber of Commerce, 350 South Second Street (Bandon) 97411: 347-9616

Coquille Chamber of Commerce, 119 North Birch Street (Coquille) 97423: 396-3414

Myrtle Point Chamber of Commerce, 424 54th Street (Myrtle Point) 97458: 572-2626

11 ~

The Covered Bridges Loop

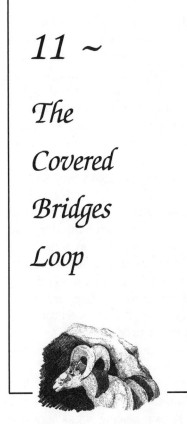

From I-5 start in Albany with a tour of the historic homes and get a covered bridge brochure from the Albany Chamber of Commerce. Follow its directions east on US 20 to State 226 on the loop that brings you back to Albany or Salem, depending on how many bridges you choose to see.

Highlights: *In addition to this cluster of five covered bridges, you will see the historic town of Albany and the heart of Oregon's famed Willamette Valley.*

It took me several attempts before I could decide on which routes to suggest through the Willamette Valley, one of my favorite parts of Oregon. The valley has so many facets to it that I couldn't decide. Finally I settled on two trips: this one built around a tour of several covered bridges, and the "route du vin" in the next chapter.

If you ask a farmer anywhere in the world to describe the perfect conditions for farming, their requirements would most likely fit the Willamette Valley. It is difficult to find anything seriously wrong with the valley, and it is little wonder that survivors of the trek across the continent on the

Oregon Trail thought they had found a small piece of heaven when they arrived in the broad, rolling valley with deep black soil and growing conditions unsurpassed anywhere in the world. The valley seemed designed for good living, with its low hills perfect for homes with panoramic views and forests of both evergreen and hardwood timber. Their most fervent wishes seemed to come true: Crop failures in the benign climate were virtually unknown; forests were thick with wood that made excellent building material; there was an abundance of streams with pure water and fish; and deer and elk cavorted across the landscape.

It is no surprise nearly a century and a half later that you see an occasional Chamber of Commerce sign reminding you that you're in the Eden at the end of the Oregon Trail.

More than 170 different crops are grown in the valley, including several kinds of fruit, grain, legumes, nuts (95 percent of the nation's hazelnuts are grown in Oregon), grass seed (more than 350 kinds), vegetables such as sweet corn and green beans, and a variety of other products such as mint, beets, wine grapes, and hay. It is also the nation's leader in English holly, bearded iris, and lily bulbs.

With so many crops being grown and so few visitors knowing what they were looking at when they drove past, a woman named Pat Coon began placing signs along a Willamette Valley road to identify the various crops. The response from travelers was so enthusiastic that the Agri-Business Council of Oregon adopted the project, and you'll see the signs throughout Oregon.

Before beginning this loop trip in search of covered bridges, stop for a visit in Albany, which has more historic homes than any other city in Oregon. There are more than 350 homes representing every major architectural style built in the United States since 1850, including the Eastlake style, the Queen Anne, Georgian, Second Empire, Italianate, Gothic Revival, and so on.

This happy situation resulted when both major highways through the Willamette Valley, first US 99, then I-5, bypassed Albany without destroying a single home. Nor has Albany had a serious fire, the other major destroyer of historic architecture.

The first home was built by the city founders, the brothers Walter and Thomas Monteith, who came to the Oregon Territory from Albany, New York. They first filed adjoining homestead claims, then built their house exactly astride the boundary line so each could legally say he lived on his own land, which was a requirement to "proving up" homestead claims. The house served at various times as a home, military headquarters, and even the birthplace of the Republican Party in Oregon.

Many homes that followed were much more ornate, as they reflected the fortunes made by residents who temporarily abandoned Albany for the California gold fields. One historian estimated that the returning miners brought $1 million into Albany, an enormous sum in 1849. Thus, Albany was a prosperous town almost from the beginning and has remained so. Its only major visual and olfactory flaw is a paper-products mill beside I-5 that emits a pungent odor and sometimes blocks traffic when its clouds of steam and smoke roll across the freeway.

Another occasional source of traffic tie-ups in the valley is the smoke from burning fields. Grass seed is a major crop in the valley—more seed is grown here than anywhere else in the world. Fields must be burned off each year before planting the new crop, and in spite of efforts to conduct the burning only when favorable winds are blowing, the smoke sometimes hangs like a shroud over the valley and freeway.

By taking the bridge loop trip described here, you will get a good sample of the richness of the Willamette Valley and a taste of history by tracking down the old covered bridges. If you are a true covered-bridge buff, you might want to try another similar loop trip from Cottage Grove south of Eugene.

In Albany, turn off US 20 onto State 226 and take it to Cold Springs Road, turn left and go into the town of Crabtree, then turn right on Hungry Hill Drive and go about four miles through the Hoffman Bridge, with its Gothic-style windows. It is ninety feet long and was built in 1936.

Continue on Hungry Hill Drive back to State 226, then turn left on Gilkey Road, follow it to Goar Road, turn right, and go through the Gilkey Bridge, which has exposed trusses and rounded portals. It is 120 feet long and was built in 1939.

Follow Gilkey Road to Robinson Drive, then turn right and go back on State 226 in Scio. Continue east to Richardson Gap Road and turn left to the Shimanek Bridge. It is painted

A covered bridge over the Santium River outside Cascadia

red, has squared portals, and the only louvered windows on a bridge in the area. It is 130 feet long and was built in 1966.

Stay on Richardson Gap Road and turn right on Shimanek Bridge Drive, which is the first right after going through the bridge. Follow it to State 226 again, then right on Camp Morrison Road through the Hannah Bridge, which has exposed trusses and is 105 feet long. It was built in 1936. Turn around beyond the bridge and retrace your route to Richardson Gap Road, turn left (south) on it and go about five miles to Larwood Drive.

Turn left on Larwood Drive and follow it about five miles to Larwood Bridge and the small park with a picnic area and partially restored waterwheel. This bridge, built in 1939, has exposed trusses and is 103 feet long. Drive west on Fish Hatchery Road to return to Crabtree and I-5. Near the bridge the Roaring River empties into Crabtree Creek. According to *Ripley's Believe It or Not*, this is the only place in the country where a river empties into a creek.

The survival of these bridges is largely the result of work by the Covered Bridge Society of Oregon, founded in 1978 to preserve the state's few remaining bridges. In the 1930s Oregon had more than 300 covered bridges. By the 1950s fewer than 140 remained, while today only 53 exist. Some of those are in storage waiting for repairs and a proper home.

Several theories have been advanced about why the bridges were covered in the first place, but there's no great mystery. They were made of wood. Wood rots, especially in a damp climate like Oregon's, so by putting a roof over them, the beams, planks, and boards were as protected as a home or barn.

The bridges were easy to build in central and western Oregon because the raw material, mostly Douglas fir, was as easy to obtain as firewood. A few were built during the 1940s due to the shortage of steel during World War II, and some were even built into the 1960s, but the rising cost of wood

77

products and labor made the use of steel and concrete more economical in later years.

The bridges served several functions other than a means to cross a stream. They were sometimes used as public meeting places—in the days before heavy traffic, of course. They were also used as hiding places for moonshine, and robbers liked to wait in them for their victims. They were routinely used as community bulletin boards, and they made ideal places for romantic trysts.

In the Area

All numbers are within area code 503.

Albany Visitors Association, 300 Second Avenue SW
(Albany) 97321: 928-0911 or (800) 526-2256

Agri-Business Council of Oregon, 8364 S.W. Nimbus
Avenue (Beaverton) 97005: 627-0860

Covered Bridge Society of Oregon, 24595 S.W. Neill Road
(Sherwood) 97140: 628-1906

Willamette Valley Visitors Association, 420 N.W. 2nd Street
(Corvallis) 97330: (800) 526-2256

12 ~

Oregon's Route du Vin

From Corvallis follow State 99W north to McMinnville, then either continue on to Portland or take State 47 north to Forest Grove. Follow directions in text for the Yamhill County loop trip or obtain a copy of "Discover Oregon Wineries" and use its maps to set your own itinerary.

Highlights: *Some of Oregon's best wineries and rural Willamette Valley towns.*

Before you begin this trip, you should pack a few things in the car in addition to the AAA-blessed emergency items. You will need a picnic hamper with wine glasses, which you can fill with food and wine bought locally, a tablecloth to use either on picnic benches or on the ground, a tried-and-true corkscrew, a reservation in a local bed and breakfast or small hotel, and most important of all, a willingness to accept the fact that Oregon's wine is as good as California's, and in some cases is better. Oregon tends to specialize in reds, while Washington does better with whites.

Oregon's wine industry has grown rapidly in a very short time, and unlike Washington to the north, the wineries are close to the major population centers along the Willamette River so that you have what amounts to a "route du vin" along State 99W.

Perhaps too much is made in the Northwest of how grapes are grown here on the same latitude as the best vineyards in France. No doubt it helps, but it doesn't take into consideration the differences in climates and soils. This difference is so great that it makes one wonder how much this geographical accident really matters.

In Oregon you can be certain of one thing: The state has the most stringent labeling laws in America. The points to remember are that the vintage is the year the grapes were grown, and the wines must contain a minimum of 90 percent of the stated vintage. The wine must be made entirely from grapes grown in the stated area. Varietal wines must be 90 percent from the stated variety (with the exception of cabernet sauvignon which is traditionally blended). Foreign place names (i.e., Champagne) are prohibited, and since sulfur dioxide has been used in nearly all wines throughout history, federal law requires this label information.

The success of wine in the Willamette Valley is the result of the soil and the marine climate that, according to the vintners, "provides a long, warm, and gentle growing season—ideal for the cultivation of noble wine grapes and berries."

Grapes grown in the valley include Pinot noir, chardonnay, Pinot gris, Riesling, cabernet sauvignon, gewürztraminer, sauvignon blanc, and Muller-Thurgau. Wines are also made from raspberries, blackberries, and boysenberries.

One of the best places to begin a loop trip is in McMinnville, a short distance southwest of Portland in the heart of the northern Willamette Valley. It is one of those

The grape harvest

unpretentious agricultural towns that has had fame almost thrust upon it by the wine industry, but retains its hometown flavor.

It is a good idea to fill your picnic basket with the makings of lunch before leaving McMinnville. Then drive north on the two-lane State 47. To savor the countryside, don't be afraid to drive slowly and pull off occasionally to enjoy the scenery. The valley is particularly beautiful here in the foothills of the Coast Range with the peaks of the Cascades rising up in the east. You will see fields of row crops, hazelnut and plum orchards, wheat and oats, tree nurseries, and fields of tall corn and low-growing berries.

Carlton is a small town of nearly 1,000 residents with several brick buildings and a scattering of antique stores in the 1893 shops, a minishopping mall in what was once the Central Heating Plant, and the McMinnville Market Place, another shopping center in a former theater.

The first winery to visit on this route is the *Arteberry Winery*, 905 East 10th Street, in McMinnville. It was founded in 1979 and produces about 3,500 cases of Pinot noir, and also makes chardonnay, sauvignon blanc, regular white Riesling, and a sparkling white Riesling. Its tasting room is open on weekends May through December from noon to 5:00 P.M.

Panther Creek Cellars is at 455 North Irvine and was founded in 1986. It produces Pinot noir, melon, and chardonnay. It is open to the public only on the Memorial Day and Thanksgiving weekends; all other times are by appointment.

The third winery in McMinnville is the *Eyrie Vineyards* at 935 East 10th Street. The first vinifera vineyard in Yamhill County, it was founded in 1966 and its Pinot noir won acclaim in tastings in France in 1975 and 1979. It also produces Pinot gris, muscat ottonel, and Pinot meunier. The winery is open by appointment only.

Driving north from McMinnville, you can go to Lafayette, which has a large antique mall (its literature says it is the largest in Oregon) in a former schoolhouse, conveniently located near the *Chateau Benoit Winery* at 6580 Northeast Mineral Springs Road. The winery specializes in sauvignon blanc and sparkling wine as well as Pinot noir, chardonnay, and Muller-Thurgau. It is open 10:00 A.M. to 5:00 P.M. daily.

Drive north on Mineral Springs Road to Carlton-Newberg Road and follow it to State 240, turn right (east) a short distance and turn left (north) on Ribbon Ridge Road, then left on North Valley Road to *Autumn Wind Vineyard* at 15225 Northeast North Valley Road. The winery has several tables with umbrellas for your convenience. Pinot noir, chardonnay, sauvignon blanc, and Pinot blanc are produced. It is open to the public on weekends and by appointment.

Drive back to North Valley Road and follow it east to Hillside Drive to Quarter Mile Lane and the *Adelsheim Vineyard* at 22150 Northeast Quarter Mile Lane. This vineyard has been in operation since 1971 and produces Pinot noir, chardonnay, Pinot gris, Riesling, and merlot. It is open to the public only two weekends a year.

Return to State 240 and go east to Newberg, then go south on State 99W to Dundee, where you'll find the *Elk Cove* tasting room at 691 Southwest State 99W. The winery itself is located near Gaston and is also open for tasting. The tasting room in Dundee is open daily 11:00 A.M. to 5:00 P.M. from May 1 through November 20.

West of Dundee on Worden Hill Road are three neighboring wineries. *Cameron Winery*, at 8200 Worden Hill Road, which was the first in Oregon to produce a certified organic wine. It emphasizes chardonnay and Pinot noir and is open only on Thanksgiving and May Day weekends and by appointment.

Nearby is *Knudsen Erath,* one of the top producers of Pinot noir in Oregon. It also makes chardonnay, cabernet sauvignon, Riesling, and gewürztraminer. It has a park adjoining the winery with a covered eating area and barbecue facilities.

The third is *Lange Winery,* 18380 Northeast Buena Vista, with great views across the Willamette Valley to the Cascades. The winery specializes in Burgundian-style Pinot noir and chardonnay, with an increasing emphasis on Oregon Pinot gris. It is open most weekends.

The *Dundee Wine Company,* operating under the Argyle label, is at the same address, 691 State 99W, and is open the same hours. One of the newer wineries, founded in 1987, Argyle produces chardonnay and dry Riesling.

One of Oregon's most successful wineries is the *Sokol Blosser Winery* a few miles southwest in the hills overlooking Dundee. In addition to Pinot noir, Riesling, and chardonnay, Sokol Blosser also produces gewürztraminer.

From here you can drive back to Lafayette and McMinnville on State 99W, or if you've stayed out too long and forgot to make a reservation, Portland is less than thirty miles north on State 99W.

In the Area

All numbers are within area code 503.

McMinnville Chamber of Commerce, 417 North Adams Street (McMinnville) 97128: 472-6196

Oregon Winegrowers' Association, 1200 N.W. Front Avenue, Suite 400 (Portland) 97209: 228-8403 or (800)

Yamhill County Wineries Association, PO Box 871 242-2363 (outside Oregon) (McMinnville) 97128: 434-5814

1893 Shops, 406 East Third Street (McMinnville) 97128: 472-4800

McMinnville Market Place, 433 East Third Street (McMinnville) 97128: 434-5047

Adelsheim Vineyard, 22150 N.E. Quarter Mile Lane (Newberg) 97132: 538-3652

Arteberry Winery, 905 East 10th Street (McMinnville) 97128: 472-1587

Argyle, 691 State 99W (Dundee) 97115: 538-8520

Autumn Wind Vineyard, 15225 N.E. North Valley Road (Newberg) 97132: 538-6931

Cameron Winery, 8200 Worden Hill Road (Dundee) 97115: 538-0336

Chateau Benoit Winery, 6580 N.E. Mineral Springs Road (Carlton) 97111: 864-2991

Eyrie Vineyards, 935 East 10th Street (McMinnville) 97128: 472-6315

Knudsen Erath, Worden Hill Road (Dundee) 97115: 538-3318

Lange Winery, 1830 N.E. Buena Vista (Dundee) 97115: 538-6476

Panther Creek Cellars, 455 North Irvine (McMinnville) 97128: 472-8080

Sokol Blosser Winery, Sokol Blosser Lane (Dundee) 97115: 864-2282

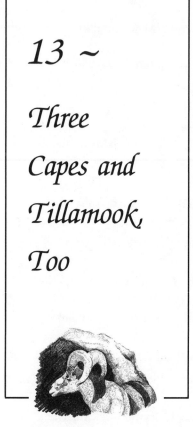

13 ~

Three Capes and Tillamook, Too

From downtown Tillamook, take the Three Capes Scenic Route, which turns west off US 101 in downtown Tillamook. Follow it to Pacific City and back to US 101 and return north to Tillamook.

Highlights: *Tillamook Bay, three capes jutting out into the Pacific, two lighthouses, rugged coastline, Cape Kiwanda, the Pacific City dory fleet, a blimp hangar museum, dairies, seafood shops, and vegetable stands.*

You may think you can drive this loop in a couple of hours, but that is only if you aren't impressed with rugged coastline, lighthouses, a boating experience unique in America, museums, and dairy and farm products. Allow yourself a full day for the trip and don't be surprised if you decide to make it last two days.

Before you arrive in Tillamook from the north, you can treat yourself to a taste of the Tillamook valley by making a few stops along US 101. The first stop will be at Debbie D's Jerky and Sausage Factory a mile north of Tillamook, where you can sample the products. Nearby you'll find the

Blue Heron French Cheese Company that produces Brie and Camembert. They also have a petting zoo outside for children.

Tillamook is a town made famous by cheese products from a dairy cooperative that has flourished in a very competitive market. The town sits in the middle of a broad valley with a generally mild and damp climate that makes for fat, contented dairy cows.

Add to this placid picture the broad and usually calm Tillamook Bay, with its excellent fishing and crabbing, and the spectacular beauty a few miles away along the coastline, and you have a great place to visit. The residents, being true northwesterners, are calm and relaxed and will try not to show their dismay if you say you'd like to move there. Oregonians have been welcoming visitors for decades, but would much prefer that they return home instead of moving in and cluttering up the natural beauty.

Your first stop will probably be the county information center on the north edge of town that shares a vast parking lot with the Tillamook Cheese factory and showroom. More than anything else, this factory is the town's identity. According to some promotional literature, it is the largest cheese factory in the world. That may or may not be accurate, but it is truly large: It produces more than forty million pounds of cheese each year.

The factory is very visitor-friendly and has a self-guided tour, plus a large gift shop and deli where you can buy a snack to take with you or eat on the premises.

The city is justifiably proud of its Tillamook County Pioneer Museum at 2106 Second Street. It is housed in the three-story former courthouse and has extensive collections of pioneer artifacts, items from World War II, guns, toys, natural history, and transportation equipment, including a stagecoach and old automobiles.

When you drive into Tillamook, watch for the Three Capes sign, which is also labeled the Netarts Highway. If you miss these two signs (highly unlikely), watch for its third name, which is Third Street. Turn right (west) and it soon takes you out of town, across the Trask River, and along the edge of Tillamook Bay on Bayocean Road.

This road was named for a disastrous housing development dating back to the turn of the century when a developer from Kansas City built a summer resort on the sandspit that juts out with the open ocean on one side and the calm Tillamook Bay on the other. He built a three-story hotel, a bowling alley, a large natatorium. He was very successful, and the town began filling up with about sixty homes.

Then the ocean began eating away at the sandspit. Soon the natatorium fell into the sea, followed by more than twenty homes. After devouring the hotel, the sea cut through nearly half a mile of sand and turned the peninsula into an island. Five homes were saved but only because they were moved. A breakwater was built in 1956 to return Bayocean to its original peninsular shape, but nobody lives there today. Everybody knows better.

Follow the signs to the Cape Meares State Park parking lot and take the short hike down to the Cape Meares lighthouse, which was first lit in 1890 and manned until it was automated in 1963. The park is a day-use area with a few picnic areas and walking trails. In addition to the lighthouse, which you can only look at from outside, the park has the "octopus tree," a very large Sitka spruce that is more than ten feet at its base and grows close to the ground rather than erect. Stories persist that the Native Americans of centuries before trained the tree to grow that way so they could store canoes in it or perhaps use it for a religious ritual.

Driving south you will go over a crest in the timber with shoulders wide enough to pull over and enjoy the view before you come to Oceanside. This is a small community of cliff dwellers whose homes look something like expensive swallows' nests. Some are old, modest summer homes and others are expensive year-round residences, all clinging to the high cliff with spectacular views of the ocean and offshore rocks.

You'll find occasional small grocery stores and cafes along the stretch between Cape Meares and Cape Lookout State Park, sometimes almost jutting out into the road. Netarts is a small collection of homes and a grocery store.

When you arrive at Lookout State Park, you are at the 700-foot level, the highest point along this route and one of the highest points along the whole Oregon coast. Like nearly every lighthouse on the coast now, Cape Lookout State Park has an automated light and the lighthouse is off-limits to visitors. The park has a beautiful campground that is sheltered from the coastal wind and rain by thick timber and bushes. The park is especially popular with bird-watchers who have counted more than 150 species of birds here.

After leaving the park you will drive over enormous sand dunes that have been stabilized somewhat by shore pine, salal, and other coastal vegetation. The highway then drops back down to sea level and goes along the shore of Sand Lake, which is actually a small bay surrounded on three sides by sand dunes. The area is popular with four-wheelers so don't expect a quiet picnic lunch at the small park on the beach.

A short distance south of here is Cape Kiwanda, which is on the northern edge of Pacific City. Cape Kiwanda is one of the most beautiful places along the coast, and Pacific City has one of the most interesting activities on any American coastline. The cape is composed of sandstone, and its colors change with the time of day and the quality of sunlight striking it. A haystack rock with a small arch carved into its northern end completes the scene. The cape was a particular favorite for Oregon's late, great landscape photographer, Ray Atkeson, who took thousands of photos there during his long career. One of his specialties was catching waves as they crashed together to create shapes that looked almost like sculpture.

Just south of the cape is a long, flat beach where the dory fishermen work, and is one of only two places in the world where fishermen launch boats in this fashion; the other is Australia. They have specially built flat-bottomed dories that are curved slightly upward at each end, something like Venetian gondolas, and they launch them at the beach from trailers. They go to sea after salmon and bottom fish, and sometimes go as far as fifty miles offshore in their open boats in pursuit of tuna.

The return is when they have all the fun. The fishermen hang around just offshore beyond the breaker line, something like surfers, waiting for the right wave. Keep a watch and you'll hear their engines as they come in at full throttle, bow up and stern down, the small boat riding on the crest of the wave. At the last moment, the fisherman shuts off the engine, hoists it clear, and skids up onto the dry sand like a demented Viking arriving in England.

This different way of going commercial fishing wasn't invented to entertain tourists. Rather it was developed when fishermen could find no other way to get out to an area just off Cape Kiwanda where they knew salmon and other food fish came close to shore. The entrance to the Nestucca River was too far away, so by trial and error the method of launching the dories and returning to shore was developed. Contrary to what you would expect, wooden dories made by local craftspeople will last for decades with the only maintenance required being an occasional fresh coat of varnish to replace that which is sanded off on the beach.

You'll find good restaurants and places to buy fresh seafood in the small, quaint Pacific City. Most of the town is strung out in a picturesque manner along the Nestucca River.

Just south of the downtown area you'll see several tall homes built on the dunes, looking something like boxy periscopes. This is the only way homes in some beach locales can have a view of the ocean. They can't be built on the unstable dunes or on the beaches because the state owns that land. So they are built with their foundations sunk into stable soil behind the line of dunes but high enough to peer out over them.

A short drive beyond Pacific City takes you to US 101, where you will turn left (north) to return to Tillamook. Your return should be a slow, leisurely one though because this stretch of highway has several things worth stopping for. Take, for example, the Bear Creek Artichokes farm near Hemlock, eleven miles south of Tillamook. As well as the obvious fare, you can buy a variety of other vegetables. They also sell herbs, flowers, and during October, thousands of pumpkins for Halloween.

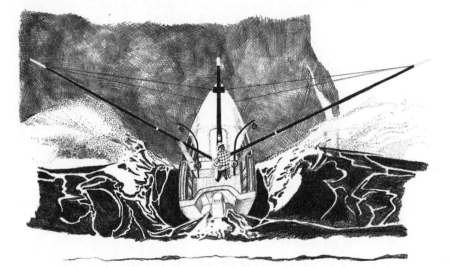

A dory fisherman struggles through the surf

About two miles south of Tillamook is an oddity left over from World War II—the Blimp Hangar Museum, which is the largest wooden clear-span building in the world. Two hangars stood out in the flatlands off US 101 until 1992, when one of them burned. The remaining hangar covers more than seven acres and could easily contain a fifteen-story building.

The two hangars were built to house eight Navy blimps each. The blimps were used during the war for antisubmarine patrol, to escort convoys of ships, and to tow targets for fighter-plane target practice. They carried depth charges, fifty-caliber machine guns, and a Browning automatic rifle. These lighter-than-air-ships were in the K-series and were 251 feet long and 58 feet in diameter. The blimps were quite successful and only one accident occurred that claimed lives. The aircraft has always had its proponents and has even been used successfully in logging.

The museum is open daily through the summer months and on weekends and holidays the rest of the year. An admission is charged.

In the Area

All numbers are within area code 503.

Tillamook Chamber of Commerce, 3705 US 101 (Tillamook) 97141: 842-7525

Tillamook Cheese, 3700 US 101 (Tillamook) 97141: 842-4481

Tillamook County Pioneer Museum, 2106 Second Street (Tillamook) 97141: 842-4553

Blimp Hangar Museum, 4000 Blimp Boulevard (Tillamook) 97141: 842-1130

Pacific City Chamber of Commerce, PO Box 331 (Pacific City) 97135: 965-6161

14 ~

The Northwest Corner

From Portland, take US 30 to Scappoose, St. Helens, Rainier, Clatskanie, Westport, Knappa, and Astoria. From Astoria, go to Fort Stevens State Park, Fort Clatsop National Monument, and follow State 202 over the Coast Range to US 26.

Highlights: *The Lower Columbia River with its series of islands and sloughs, the seagoing ship and tug traffic, historic mansions and museums, a fort fired on by a Japanese submarine during World War II, a replica of Lewis and Clark's camp, and a drive over the Coast Range.*

From Bonneville Dam in the Columbia Gorge down to the Pacific Ocean beyond Astoria, the Columbia River changes character. It now is a seafaring river and subject to the ebb and flow of the tides; the tidal effect would go farther upstream were it not for the dam. From Portland to the sea you will often notice—or at least imagine—a saltwater tang in the air. The steady line of ships coming in from the Pacific Rim to Portland, Kalama, Longview, and Astoria makes it as much a seaway as a river.

The Columbia becomes a very large river after it joins the Willamette River behind Sauvie Island. Then it picks up the

Lewis and Cowlitz rivers which add considerably to its volume, and when it reaches Astoria it is more than four miles wide in places.

The drive downriver from Portland is a favorite with river rats because you can see the river as you drive along and enjoy the ships, boats, and the rows of piling jutting out into the river with enormous log booms tied to them, waiting for their turn at the pulp and paper mills. Sometimes booms are allowed to sit anchored for several months, long enough for weeds and brush to take root on the logs, making the boom look like a small island.

The larger Lower Columbia towns are all on the Washington side, mainly because of the large rivers—the Lewis and the Cowlitz—that drain down from the Cascade Range. This leaves the Oregon side with smaller, more intimate towns, such as Scappoose, which has several antique stores, and St. Helens, where you'll find the Columbia County Historical Society Museum with a good collection of marine artifacts and a handsome collection of Native American photographs.

Near Rainier you'll pass the Trojan Nuclear Power Plant, the first and only nuclear power plant in Oregon. As this was being written, plans were under way to close and perhaps dismantle the plant.

Immediately after you pass Rainier, the highway begins its climb to the top of the bluffs that line the river for the next several miles. At the top of the hill is a turnout with views across the river to the Washington side. The highway cuts inland from the summit and goes through thick timber and an occasional clearing for farms. A side road leads back to the river at Mayger and loops back around to return to US 30 at Clatskanie.

Clatskanie is a small, pretty town with a few historic buildings, including the Flippin House, sometimes called the

Castle. It is a turreted Victorian home now used as the local senior citizen center.

A few miles on to the west is Westport, where a small ferry runs back and forth to Washington's Puget Island. The highway climbs to the summit of a hill where the Bradley Wayside State Park has a good view of the river valley and Puget Island almost directly below. In the early 1960s, an acre-size piece of the hill fell off into the river, creating a wave that swept over part of Puget Island and killed at least one person.

The rest of the drive to Astoria is uneventful until just before you arrive at the city limits. Just east of Astoria, around the small town of Swensen, the timber suddenly seems to close in on the road, and it seems to always be wet and a little dark here—imagination at work perhaps, but that has been my experience every time I drive this route. The river comes back into view, and you'll see several picturesque houseboats afloat in sloughs and fishing boats of all descriptions tied to the bank or to old piling.

Watch for Tongue Point, a peninsula that juts out into the Columbia River just past Swensen. It used to be a military post with miles of piers sticking out into the river to which liberty ships from World War II were moored. In recent years Tongue Point has been turned into a Coast Guard station and a Job Corps center, along with a few other similar uses. The liberty ships were towed away and reduced to scrap metal, and the long piers stand empty and useless.

You will see hundreds of small commercial fishing boats around the Astoria area because this is one of the most important salmon-fishing areas in Oregon. Almost all the boats have a large drum on the front or stern, which means they are

gill-netters. Fishermen string the net out with a float and a light on the end. The net has floats on one edge and weights on the other, which makes it hang like a curtain behind the boat. When the net is out behind the boat, it is called a drift. Salmon get caught in the nets, which are large enough for their heads to enter but not large enough to permit their bodies to go through. They can't back out because the net catches their gills.

Fishermen in the Astoria area have formed a way of working together that is unique in North American fishing. Groups are formed to keep a section of the river cleared of the debris that can damage nets. These groups are called snag associations. Only the fishermen who help keep the river clear of snags and other debris are permitted to set their nets in these areas.

The Astoria waterfront

Astoria is said to be the oldest permanent settlement west of the Mississippi. Its history goes back to 1811 when a fur-trading post was built by a group funded by John Jacob Astor. Only five years earlier the Lewis and Clark expedition built Fort Clatsop and spent the winter of 1804–05 a few miles away on Youngs River.

The area has long been a mecca for Scandinavians, housing a particularly large Finnish population, with radio stations broadcasting in and newspapers printed in Finnish. Not surprisingly, Astoria has several saunas. Scandinavian food is sold in grocery stores and restaurants.

Astoria is another of those pioneer towns that somehow avoided the devastating fires that regularly forced builders to switch from wood to brick. This means that Astoria has one of the best collections of Victorian and Carpenter-Gothic houses in the Northwest. The local Chamber of Commerce has maps for self-guided tours of the elegant old homes. Astoria isn't a large town, so a tour will take only a few minutes.

One of the dominant features is the Astor Column atop 595-foot Coxcomb Hill. The 125-foot tower has 166 steps inside to the top where you'll have an unsurpassed view of the region. The exterior of the circular tower is decorated with a frieze painted by an Italian artisan imported for the job. It depicts various events in Astoria's history and, according to the Chamber of Commerce, is the nation's only "large piece of memorial architecture of reinforced concrete finished with a pictorial frieze in grafitto work." The column was erected as a joint project between the Great Northern Railroad and John Jacob Astor's descendants in 1926. According to a local legend, when the special train arrived bearing the Astor scion for the event, he (or perhaps it was a she) looked over the town, didn't like the looks of it, and refused to leave the private rail car.

The Columbia River Maritime Museum on the waterfront downtown is one of the best such museums in the West. It has an enormous library, artifacts from many of the ships that foundered at the Columbia River Bar, several kinds of fishing boats and old fishing gear, and many other types of artifacts. Outside is the lightship *Columbia*, which was donated to the museum when it was no longer needed off the mouth of the river.

From Astoria, take US 101 south across the Youngs Bay Bridge and turn right on the Fort Stevens Highway, which leads to Fort Stevens State Park, one of the most popular in Oregon's large system and certainly one with a great history. It was formerly an army post, the southern counterpart to Fort

Columbia, which guarded the northern side of the river from invasion. The forts were equipped with the odd ten-inch disappearing rifles, which were cannons that, when fired, swung down out of the line of fire to be reloaded.

The fort's main claim to fame, though, is that it was fired on by a Japanese submarine on the night of June 21, 1942. The submarine fired seventeen shells toward the battery, trying to draw its fire so the submarine's guns could be sighted in on the battery. The battery's guns weren't powerful enough to fire beyond the high-tide line (the beach had grown farther and farther out into the ocean after the jetties were built on either side of the river to direct the flow). Knowing this, the battery commander ordered his men to hold their fire. The submarine had to give up and go away.

Nearby on the beach is the wreck of the *Peter Iredale*, an iron-clad, four-masted British barkentine that ran aground on October 25, 1906. This is something of a symbol for the Columbia estuary, known throughout the world as the "Graveyard of the Pacific." The remains of the ship will probably last for several more decades, but the sea is gradually eroding the ribs and hull. Several parts of the ship, including the bowsprit, are preserved in the Columbia River Maritime Museum.

The third major site here is Fort Clatsop National Memorial, a short distance south of US 101, where the thirty-three-member Lewis and Clark party spent the winter of 1805–06 after coming to the Pacific Ocean from St. Louis. In 1955 a group of residents set out to find the exact location of the fort, and through archaeological digging, found enough corner post stubs—the original buildings had been burned—to establish the perimeters of the fort. Using sketches from the explorers' journals, a replica was built. Three years later the Fort Clatsop National Memorial was created by Congress. The memorial is open every day except Christmas, and during the busy summer months rangers dressed in period costumes show how the explorers lived and give demonstrations in candle making, tanning and sewing hides, woodworking, and firing muzzle-loading rifles.

From Fort Clatsop return to Astoria via US 101 and turn right on State 202, which is also Marine Drive, and follow Youngs River upstream. You'll pass lots of abandoned piling along the riverbank, and the ubiquitous gill net fishing boats are tied to private docks or old piling or are pulled up on blocks.

The highway quickly becomes crooked as it passes small farms before entering the forest of the Coast Range. Most of this forest land is privately owned and has been logged extensively over the years. Very little, if any, old-growth trees remain standing, and you'll pass many clear-cut patches where some usable wood was left lying on the ground. You'll also see examples of clear-cut land that has been replanted, the new trees growing uniformly like a deep carpet across the mountains.

Few issues are more emotional in the Northwest than the controversy involving the spotted owl and clear-cutting. If you love the outdoors, it is difficult not to become emotional about clear-cutting. However, it should also be remembered that this land is privately owned, and its owners can legally do almost anything they want with it. Also, in order to produce furniture, houses, paper, and a myriad of other wood-based products, trees have to be cut. Chopping down trees is not a beautiful act, but it is an emotional issue in any area where logging is a primary source of income.

The highway winds its way through the timber, crossing Youngs River again and again as it gets smaller and smaller the higher you go. You'll see lots of Douglas fir, of course, but also cedar, spruce, groves of almost-white alder, and the usual coastal underbrush of salal, various berries, and an occasional wild rhododendron.

The only town on this route is Jewell, which has a cluster of buildings and the consolidated grade and high schools. A short distance beyond Jewell is the Jewell Meadows Wildlife Refuge, the one place in this part of Oregon where you can be almost certain to see wildlife. The refuge was established to provide food and safety for the local herd of elk and deer that share the forest. It isn't unusual to see more than 100 head of elk and a lesser number of deer contentedly grazing in the large, sloping meadow. You'll also see many species of birds that have joined the animals in the safe zone.

It is less than ten miles from the refuge to the busy US 26, which you can take to Portland or back to the beach communities of Cannon Beach and Seaside.

In the Area

All numbers are within area code 503.

Columbia County Historical Society Museum, Strand Street (St. Helens) 97051: 397-4322

Clatskanie Chamber of Commerce, PO Box 635 (Clatskanie) 97016: 728-2502

Astoria Chamber of Commerce, 111 West Marine Drive (Astoria) 97103: 325-6311

Columbia River Maritime Museum, 1792 Marine Drive (Astoria) 97103: 325-2323

Clatsop County Historical Society Museum, 1618 Exchange Street (Astoria) 97103: 325-2203

Fort Stevens State Park (Hammond) 97121: 861-2000

Fort Clatsop National Memorial, Route 3, Box 604-FC (Astoria) 97103: 861-2471.

Jewell Meadows Wildlife Area (Jewell) Information: Oregon Department of Fish & Wildlife, PO Box 59 (Portland) 97207: 229-5403

15 ~

The Columbia Gorge

From Portland, take I-84 east to Troutdale, turn right to US 30 and follow the Historic Columbia River Highway signs to The Dalles. Only portions of the highway are open, so you may want to drive only the thirty-mile stretch from Troutdale to John B. Yeon State Park.

Highlights: *Easily among the top ten scenic highways in America, this trip takes you to many scenic overlooks, past more than seventy waterfalls, historic buildings, orchards, dams, and a wide variety of boats on the Columbia River.*

The Columbia River Gorge is so beautiful and has such a variety of beauty that it has been known to strike writers mute who are normally prolific. It has a little of everything, from desert to rain forest topography, and a lot of rugged natural beauty.

The gorge is the only gap in the Cascade Range between its northern end in British Columbia and its southern terminus in northern California. This gap permits the Columbia River to run almost due west for more than 100 miles, much of it within the 292,000-acre Columbia River Gorge National Scenic Area created in 1986.

In actuality, the Columbia River doesn't really run or flow here, because it is little more than a lake behind a series of dams all the way along the river, from Canada to Bonneville Dam, the last of a series built to generate electricity. Before the dams, the river was the wildest of the big rivers in America. It had a series of rapids, waterfalls, and whirlpools through the gorge. Rail lines were built to transport freight and passengers around the worst obstacles to steamboats, and locks were carved out of the canyon to permit boats to go around others.

One of the greatest losses to modern technology was Celilo Falls, where for centuries Native Americans had built platforms out over the thundering falls and stood on the rickety platforms to snare migrating salmon with nets. Today Celilo Falls, like the Cascades and the stepping-stone rapids at The Dalles, is nothing more than submerged rocks.

Interestingly, the Columbia Gorge is one of the few scenic places where the highway was built to complement the natural setting and as a result is considered a thing of beauty. That's because much of the highway was a private enterprise built by stone masons under the direction of a pioneering road builder named Sam Lancaster who toured Europe to learn the road-building techniques that made so many beautiful roads there. The instigator of the whole thing, though, was a wealthy philanthropist named Samuel C. Hill, an attorney in Seattle who built the mansion downriver in Maryhill that became a major museum and the peace arch on the U.S.-Canadian border at Blaine. He was deeply involved in restoring Europe after World War I and was a son-in-law of the railroad tycoon, James J. Hill.

Hill believed more strongly than most in the future of automobiles and led the campaign to finance the highway with private funds, telling audiences that "there are thirty Switzerlands in Oregon," and was able to attract funding from some of the Northwest's most wealthy families. This led to the creation in 1913 of the Oregon State Highway Department and Commission.

Construction of the highway began in October 1913. Lancaster designed it to make use of dry masonry walls, built by Italian artisans imported for the work, and rubble guard rails with arched openings. At Mitchell Point the builders blasted out five tunnels to exceed the three-tunnel Axenstrasse around Lake Lucerne in Switzerland. Completed on July 6, 1915, the unpaved road between Portland and Hood River attracted sightseers who immediately clogged the new, yet primitive highway.

The following year voters approved a referendum to pay for paving the road, and on June 7, 1916, President Woodrow Wilson touched a button in the White House that electrically unfurled the American flag at the Crown Point observatory. Even the British were impressed: The *Illustrated London News* proclaimed it the King of Roads.

The highway had many years of supremacy but became a poor cousin to I-84 which was built at water level in the 1950s. Parts of the old highway were closed entirely, and one of the major tunnels was dynamited shut. During the 1980s, with the trend toward beautification and environmental protection, restoration of the highway became a popular cause along with preserving the natural beauty of the gorge. The state highway department is investing millions of dollars in this restoration, and it is expected to be completed by the turn of the century.

For the time being, you can catch bits and pieces of it by leaving the speedy I-84 in favor of leisurely driving along the edge of cliffs and past farms and orchards. Start by driving to Troutdale, about fifteen miles east of I-205, and follow the Historic Columbia River Highway logo signs through Troutdale, a quiet and small town with many buildings dating back to its heyday when the old highway took all traffic down its main drag.

When you cross the Sandy River Bridge, you enter the Columbia Gorge National Scenic Area which is jointly managed by the Forest Service, Oregon, Washington, and the six counties involved. The highway follows the Sandy River to the south, upstream, to reach the high plateau where you'll see new wooden guard rails being installed to match the originals.

The highway runs through two small and quiet towns, Springdale and Corbett, then reaches the first of several spectacular viewpoints, Chanticleer Point. Here the Portland Women's Forum donated the viewpoint overlooking the gorge and Larch Mountain. Nearby is the site of the Chanticleer Inn, which the highway founders used as a meeting place to plan the construction. The inn burned in the 1930s.

The highway descends to perhaps the most photographed spot along the gorge, the Vista House at Crown Point State Park. The domed observatory was designed by a Portland architect, Edgar M. Lazarus, who later wrote that he designed it to "recall the ancient and mystic Thor's Crown for which the point was originally named." The house is used as an interpretive site and gift shop during the summer season.

Immediately after leaving Crown Point, the highway becomes extremely crooked as it winds its way downward. The designer, Sam Lancaster, planned it so that the maximum grade would be 5 percent and the curve radii would be no more than 100 feet. As it drops the 600 feet, it parallels itself five times as it enters the rain forest at river level and soon passes Latourell Falls, which is 249 feet high. The best view of the falls is from the bridge across Latourell Creek.

Shepperd's Dell State Park is next with a trail leading back to a spot where it is said the former owner of the property, George Shepperd, took his family for spiritual refreshment

Columbia Gorge

when they couldn't attend church. He later donated the land to the people of Portland, and it eventually became a state park.

East of the park are a series of landmarks along the highway. First is a three-hipped barn on the north side of the highway built in 1870. On the south side is a 1929 English cottage-style home. A short distance farther is the Forrest Hall, a Georgian-style building that once housed a restaurant, and half a mile beyond that is the Bridal Veil Inn, which was built after the original highway opened and is still in business.

Bridal Veil is an area that includes a lumber mill by that name, a town, a creek, a popular waterfall, and the Bridal Veil State Park. However, "the" waterfall of the Columbia Gorge is

Multnomah Falls. At 620 feet, it is by far the highest in the gorge and reportedly the second highest year-round waterfall in the United States. Sam Lancaster, the highway builder, put it better than anyone: "There are higher waterfalls and falls of greater volume, but there are none more beautiful than Multnomah."

According to highway folklore, Lancaster was talking to one of the principal backers, Simon Benson (who built the Benson Hotel in Portland and the Columbia Gorge Hotel just outside Hood River), and one of them said it would be nice to have a footbridge across the lower waterfall. Benson wrote a check for it on the spot.

Another area as beautiful in its own way is the hike up Oneonita Creek through the small gorge to a waterfall that seems to be pouring out of a bowl into the narrow chasm. The little gorge is so cool the year-round that it nurtures a botanical section unlike any other in the area. Be sure and bring your camera to Oneonita Falls and be forewarned that the sun hits the falls only a few hours in midday. The next waterfall is Horsetail Falls, 176 feet high, which can be seen from a bridge over Horsetail Creek.

This portion of the highway ends at John B. Yeon State Park, and only bits and pieces, some less than a mile long, remain until you reach Mosier. One section worth taking is at the Eagle Creek Park exit. There you'll find a tunnel and the Eagle Creek Bridge faced with native stone. The bridge also has a stone guardrail and pedestrian observatory.

Another long section begins near Mosier, just east of Hood River, and is notable for the Rowena Loops, a series of switchbacks that is another example of Lancaster's rule against steep grades. He obviously had nothing against crooked roads, however.

Along the area between Hood River and The Dalles, you will usually see swarms of windsurfers out in the river, like a flock of one-winged butterflies. The Columbia Gorge is considered one of the best windsurfing places in the world and has hosted world championships.

Windsurfers can be seen whipping back and forth in front of and around barges being pushed up and down the river by towboats. In one of those maritime oddities, towboats push rather than pull their loads along as their name would indicate. The towboats are so much more economical to operate than trains and trucks that they are used to move much of the wheat and other grain from eastern Oregon, Washington, and Idaho to ports along the Lower Columbia.

The historical highway officially ends at the western end of The Dalles when it crosses Chenoweth Creek, although the road obviously continues into downtown The Dalles. The eastern end of the Columbia Gorge is difficult to identify because the desert landscape of exposed basalt and canyon topography continues on to the Tri-Cities area of Washington. Biggs, where US 97 crosses the Columbia River, is as good as any place to end the gorge drive. Here you can go south into central Oregon, north into Washington, or turn around and rush back to Portland on the four-lane I-84.

In the Area

All numbers are within area code 503.

Historic Preservation League of Oregon, PO Box 40053
    (Portland) 97240: 243-1923

Troutdale Chamber of Commerce, PO Box 245 (Troutdale)
    97060: 669-7473

Hood River Chamber of Commerce, Port Marina Park
    (Hood River) 97031: 386-2000

The Dalles Chamber of Commerce, 404 West 2nd Street
    (The Dalles) 97058: 296-2231

Forest Service Columbia Gorge Ranger Station, 31520 S.E. Woodard Road (Troutdale) 97230: 695-2276

Columbia River Gorge National Scenic Area, 902 Wasco Avenue (Hood River) 97031: 386-2333

Columbia Gorge Hotel, 4000 Westcliff Drive (Hood River) 97031: 386-3359

Bibliography

Applegate, Shannon. *Skookum*. New York: William Morrow, 1988.

Armstrong, Chester H. *Oregon State Parks History 1917–1963*.

Brown, Wilfred H. *This Was a Man*. North Hollywood, California: The Camas Press, 1971.

Cantwell, Robert. *The Hidden Northwest*. Philadelphia: J. B. Lippincott, 1972.

Cogswell, Philip, Jr. *Capitol Names*. Portland: Oregon Historical Society, 1977.

Friedman, Ralph. *A Touch of Oregon*. New York: Ballantine Books, 1970.

Friedman, Ralph. *In Search of Western Oregon*. Caldwell, Idaho: Caxton Printers, 1990.

Green, Stewart M. *Back Country Byways*. Helena and Billings, Montana: Falcon Press, 1991.

Gulick, Bill. *Roadside History of Oregon*. Missoula, Montana: Mountain Press, 1991.

Jackman, E. R., and Long, R. A. *The Oregon Desert*. Caldwell, Idaho: Caxton Printers, 1967.

Schwartz, Susan. *Nature in the Northwest*. Englewood Cliffs, New Jersey: Prentice-Hall, 1983.

Warren, Stuart, and Ishikawa, Ted Long. *The Oregon Handbook.* Chico, California: Moon Publications, 1991.

Weis, Norman D. *Ghost Towns of the Northwest.* Caldwell, Idaho: Caxton Printers, 1971.

Works Projects Administration, *Oregon.* Portland, Oregon: Binfords & Mort.

Index

Index

Other titles in the Country Roads Series:

Country Roads of Indiana
Country Roads of Illinois
Country Roads of Michigan
Country Roads of Massachusetts
Country Roads of Kentucky
Country Roads of New Hampshire
Country Roads of Ohio
Country Roads of Pennsylvania
Country Roads of Hawaii
Country Roads of New York
Country Days in New York City
Country Roads of Vermont
Country Roads of Quebec
Country Roads of Oregon
Country Roads of Washington

All books are $9.95 at bookstores.
Or order directly from the publisher (add $3.00
shipping & handling for direct orders):

Country Roads Press
P.O. Box 286
Castine, Maine 04421
Toll-free order number: **800-729-9179**